DISCARDED

PRENTICE-HALL
CONTEMPORARY PERSPECTIVES IN MUSIC EDUCATION SERIES
Charles Leonhard, Editor

Bennett Reimer
A PHILOSOPHY OF MUSIC EDUCATION

Robert Sidnell
BUILDING INSTRUCTIONAL PROGRAMS IN MUSIC EDUCATION

Charles Leonhard
THE ROLE OF METHOD IN MUSIC EDUCATION

Edwin Gordon
THE PSYCHOLOGY OF MUSIC TEACHING

Robert House
ADMINISTRATION IN MUSIC EDUCATION

Richard Colwell
THE EVALUATION OF MUSIC TEACHING AND LEARNING

Clifford K. Madsen and Charles H. Madsen, Jr.
EXPERIMENTAL RESEARCH IN MUSIC

Daniel L. Wilmot
IMPROVING INSTRUCTION IN MUSIC EDUCATION

ADMINISTRATION IN MUSIC EDUCATION

PRENTICE-HALL INTERNATIONAL, INC., *London*
PRENTICE-HALL OF AUSTRALIA, PTY. LTD., *Sydney*
PRENTICE-HALL OF CANADA, LTD., *Toronto*
PRENTICE-HALL OF INDIA PRIVATE LIMITED, *New Delhi*
PRENTICE-HALL OF JAPAN, INC., *Tokyo*

administration
in music education

ROBERT W. HOUSE
Director, School of Music
Southern Illinois University

PRENTICE-HALL, INC., Englewood Cliffs, New Jersey

Library of Congress Cataloging in Publication Data

HOUSE, ROBERT WILLIAM.
    Administration in music education.

    (Prentice-Hall contemporary perspectives in music
education series)
    Includes bibliographies.
    1. School music-Instruction and study.   2. School
management and organization.   I. Title.
MT1.H84   780.72   72–4564
ISBN   0-13-005140-3
ISBN   0-13-005132-0 (pbk.)

780.72
H81a
82962
apr. 1973

© 1973 by PRENTICE-HALL, INC., Englewood Cliffs, New Jersey

        Printed in the United States of America

        10   9   8   7   6   5   4   3   2   1

foreword

Contemporary Perspectives in Music Education is a new series of professional books for music education. It establishes a pattern for music teacher education based on the areas of knowledge and processes involved in music education rather than on the levels and specializations in music education.

The areas of knowledge include philosophy of music education, psychology of music teaching, and research methods. The processes include program development, instruction, administration, supervision, and evaluation.

The basic premise of the series is that mastery of all of these processes and areas of knowledge is essential for the successful music educator regardless of his area of specialization and the level at which he teaches. The series presents in a systematic fashion information and concepts basic to a unified music education profession.

All of the books in the series have been designed and written for use in the undergraduate program of music teacher education. The pattern of the series is both systematic and flexible. It permits music education instructors at the college level to select one or more of the books as texts on the basis of their relevance to a particular course.

Administration, the process which has as its purpose the provision of the setting for learning, is a matter of concern to all music educators. All music educators, whatever their primary responsibility, have a role in the administration of the music program. As a consequence, all music educators need to understand the process of administration and to perceive accurately their role as well as that of music leadership personnel in providing the setting for musical learning. Professor House's book, the first to deal with music administration as a discrete process, is expressly designed to fill that need.

Professor House is uniquely qualified to write an authoritative book on the administration of music programs. He has had long and successful experience as a music administrator and has given the process of administration serious and thorough study. His mastery of both the theory and practice of administration has resulted in a book that will be of great value both to students preparing to become music educators and to practicing music teachers and administrators.

As the music program becomes more complex and sophisticated, the administration of it requires music teachers and leadership personnel who are knowledgeable and skilled in administrative technique. As a source of that knowledge and skill, this book will make a real contribution to the development of a higher level of professionalism among music educators.

Charles Leonhard

preface

The administrative role in music education has generally been learned by trial and error, and has only recently attracted any widespread attention. Those publications which do exist tend to view the task chiefly through the eyes of the public school music supervisor.

Chapter Nine of *Foundations and Principles of Music Education,* by Charles Leonhard and Robert House, established some general principles pertaining to administration in music education. It is this book's purpose to expand on that beginning. Principles have been applied from the fields of educational administration and business management, as well as materials based upon normal practice in the discipline of music. The attempt has been to build a universal approach, covering all the administrative aspects of music programs in the elementary and secondary schools and colleges. Such an approach should be of value to all music teachers as well as to their supervisors and department chairmen, and to their principals, deans, and superintendents as well, in helping them achieve a useful conception of the process of management applied to the field of music education.

The author draws upon over twenty years' experience as a music administrator in educational institutions. He has worked at small, medium, and large sized universities and has been involved continually with elementary and secondary music programs. He has also served quite actively for the accrediting agencies, in evaluating music programs at all levels. It is his hope that this publication will overcome misconceptions of the administrative role in music education, and serve to widen and deepen the understanding of that task.

R.H.

contents

CHAPTER ONE

the nature of educational administration   *1*

THE FUNCTION OF SCHOOLING   *4*
TYPES AND LEVELS OF SCHOOLING   *10*
CONCEPTS OF EDUCATIONAL ADMINISTRATION   *14*
THE QUALITIES OF SUCCESSFUL ADMINISTRATION   *15*
SUGGESTED READINGS   *19*

CHAPTER TWO

administrative roles and the music program   *20*

ADMINISTRATION, SUPERVISION, AND INSTRUCTION   *20*
THE MANAGEMENT PROCESS   *21*
ADMINISTRATIVE ROLES   *33*
ADMINISTRATIVE LEADERSHIP   *41*
SUGGESTED READINGS   *46*

xi

CHAPTER THREE

building the music curriculum   47

DEVELOPING OBJECTIVES   *48*

ESTABLISHING OFFERINGS AND REQUIREMENTS   *53*

EXPEDITING INSTRUCTION   *65*

EVALUATION OF THE MUSIC CURRICULUM   *71*

SUGGESTED READINGS   *74*

CHAPTER FOUR

music faculty development   76

FACULTY RECRUITMENT AND SELECTION   *77*

ASSIGNMENT   *81*

ORIENTATION   *82*

FACULTY COMMUNICATION AND MORALE   *83*

EVALUATION   *85*

SUGGESTED READINGS   *91*

CHAPTER FIVE

working with music students   92

THE STUDENT POPULATION   *92*

RECRUITMENT FOR MUSIC   *95*

ADVISEMENT AND COUNSELING   *98*

RESOURCE SERVICES   *102*

STUDENT COMMUNICATION AND BEHAVIOR   *104*

PROMOTING SCHOLARSHIP AND MUSICIANSHIP   *106*

EVALUATION   *107*

STUDENT RECORDS   *109*

SUGGESTED READINGS   *110*

CHAPTER SIX

fiscal management   111

FINANCING   *112*

BUDGETING   *117*

PROCURING GOODS AND SERVICES   *125*

FINANCIAL ACCOUNTING   *127*

PROTECTING FUNDS, PROPERTY, AND PERSONS   *129*

SUGGESTED READINGS   *131*

CHAPTER SEVEN

providing music facilities   *133*

MUSIC ROOMS   *134*

UTILIZING AND SECURING SPACE   *141*

PLANNING NEW FACILITIES   *143*

EQUIPMENT   *144*

USE AND MAINTENANCE OF FACILITIES   *146*

SUGGESTED READINGS   *149*

CHAPTER EIGHT

area and continuing services in music   *150*

COMMUNITY SERVICES   *151*

COMMUNICATIONS   *153*

ALUMNI SERVICES   *156*

SUGGESTED READINGS   *164*

index   *167*

ADMINISTRATION IN MUSIC EDUCATION

CHAPTER ONE

the nature of educational administration

This book is intended to be of especial value to music educators and future music educators who need to develop more understanding of the administrative process and how it affects them. Many are destined to undertake clear-cut administrative roles; the others will necessarily be working constantly with school administrators and will often find themselves assuming administrative tasks. In truth, the line between teacher and administrator is quite blurred. School administration means, simply, providing the means of instruction. Thus, all music educators share to some extent in the administrative task as they assist in developing the proper combination of students and teachers, curriculum, and physical properties in order to achieve useful musical learning.

Some posts, however, carry specific administrative responsibilities. By way of preliminary identification, we are speaking of school superintendents and their assistants, building principals, subject matter supervisors and consultants, and directors of specific school activities or services such as instrumental and choral organizations, athletics, cafeterias, counseling, business affairs, etc. Different titles are used at the university level, such as president, chancellor, dean, department chairman, and the like. Members of governing boards such as local school boards and boards of trustees are also considered to be part of the administrative chain.

Part of the problem in studying the administrative side of education lies in the negative attitudes of many school people toward administrators. The following stereotypes are typical:

1. The administrator is "the boss." He hires and fires and his judgment is not to be questioned openly. In fact, he will expect special consideration and deference to his opinions.

2. Administrators form a privileged oligarchy, separate from other school personnel. They have certain prerogatives and high salaries, which they are anxious to protect. Their instinctive mode of conduct is to "play it close to the chest" and to close ranks when questioned. Thus, it is compromising to have too much social contact with them, to belong to the same union, or to accept administrative policy at face value.

3. The administrator is simply the man who holds the purse strings. Since "the squeaking wheel gets the grease," it is good tactics to see one's administrator on frequent occasions and always have some new item to request.

4. Administrators may once have been musicians and educators, but long disuse has blunted their skills so they have sunk to the level of mere paper shufflers. Consequently, they are no longer competent to deal with significant policy formation. Their proper role is to carry out operations already outlined by the teaching faculty.

These stereotypes are not without foundation. Many readers will recognize their own attitudes, based upon direct observation and experience with certain administrators. But these are not inherent qualities of the job; there are numerous examples of effective administrative operation which can be duplicated wherever the task is properly understood and good people are obtained to do it.

Actually, we suspect that many administrators are misjudged. They do make handy scapegoats, but it is manifestly unfair to blame them for inability to control external influences and for failing to anticipate every problem that may arise.

What is true is that the administrative function cannot be properly exercised without a tinge of paternalism—since the job is to provide and facilitate, to protect and direct—and thus the administrator is regarded with ambivalent feelings. He is expected to nurture a new program to maturity and then to stand aside, to provide all needed tools to instruction but not to nag the teacher about their care and use. The problems are compounded in these times because the administrator is supposed to conduct his activity in a goldfish bowl with "full communication" and "accountability." His constituency—teachers and students, parents and taxpayers—expect to look over his shoulder while he works. Thus, the tenure of university presidents and other top administrators is becoming shorter each year.

Fortunately, in these days of political strife and educational re-examination, the music programs in schools and colleges are not often under direct fire. Indeed, the arts and humanities are currently favored by youth in their reaction against war, technology, and materialism. Administering a school music program, therefore, is more likely to offer problems in overcoming its neglect, rather than in crisis management. Even so, pressures from the youth for more attention to guitars and rock music and for more involvement in decision-making must be faced. And when this phase is passed there will be another. The music administrator is navigating a moving ship and can never relax his vigilance.

The topic of educational administration seems grossly neglected, possibly because of the great preoccupation with the processes of learning and instruction. But the logistic problems of school should be of great concern to all if maximum results are to be obtained. To teach music one must recruit and organize the students, determine where and when they are to meet together, secure the necessary equipment, and provide the compositions which are to be studied and rehearsed. It is often said, "much must be done before giving the downbeat."

All this preparation for instruction is in the administrative realm, but the reader should not secure the impression that good administration consists simply in pouring people and equipment together in the classroom. Effective administration coordinates efforts toward the goals of the organization—which goal in this case is partially defined in terms of the musical learning of the students. The relationship has been graphically illustrated in Handbook VI of the U.S. Office of Education, showing how the administration surrounds and supports the instructional efforts and points toward the objectives of the school.[1]

Although the broad purpose of educational administration is thus clear—to facilitate learning and instruction—a useful understanding of its application in the field of music education is not simple to attain. One must reexamine the larger purposes of schooling, the relationship of music to other subjects within the curriculum, and the particular task to be accomplished at each level of schooling. One must also have a working concept of all the elements affecting instruction and the kinds of roles assigned to various individuals. Finally, one can examine operational problems involved in the music program from an administrative viewpoint. From this kind of study, one should be able to handle administrative tasks more effectively within his own sector of the music

---

[1] *Standard Terminology for Curriculum and Instruction in Local and State School Systems,* U.S. Government Printing Office, Washington, D.C., 1970, p. 2.

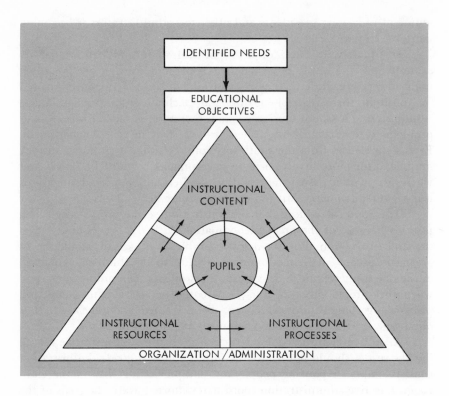

program and to work more positively with the various school officials in the service of music education.

THE FUNCTION OF SCHOOLING

The reader should notice that a careful distinction is made between *education* and *schooling*. Education results from adaptive behavior in response to environmental pressures; schooling is formal, organized education. Schools are provided by various agencies in our society to produce in individuals the kinds of knowledge and skills that are thought to be necessary. Thus, the church school is meant to inculcate the faith; the English public (i.e., private) school is designed to deliver traits believed to be desirable in upper class English society; the American common school hopes to produce democratically-inclined individuals, capable of self-government.

The purposes of a school, therefore, are defined by those who establish it and support it and are naturally influenced by the interpretations of its faculty and by the reactions of its students. By and large, those schools which are attended by a mass of undifferentiated citizenry are going to stress "general education," or those elements of knowledge and skill thought to be essential for all. Schools catering to future teachers, musicians, medical doctors, or debutantes will view their purposes accordingly.

In any case, schooling is designed to complement education, for we all become educated largely by means of natural forces in and around us. Understanding and skill in popular music, for example, hardly depends upon what is offered in the schools, although the study of such literature in schools is certainly legitimate if the study is structured in such a way as to promote certain objectives of the school.

A school is obviously concerned with giving the student something special which he needs but probably would not acquire outside its walls. This "something" is the "curriculum," which includes all the experiences undergone by the students within the school. It is the means by which the school attempts to achieve its purposes. It derives from the subjects offered and their content, the school activities and clubs, the library services, the counseling and health programs, and all the procedures and attitudes that prevail among the student body and faculty.

Although all schools do not share equally in the responsibility, an overriding necessity exists to provide effective general education to all students. This is normally taken to include the basic elements of written and spoken English, mathematics, natural and social sciences, the fine and applied arts; however, opinion varies greatly as to the actual kinds and levels of abilities that it is necessary to produce. The idea is that all content must meet these two tests:

1. Is the information or ability useful to all?
2. Is it something that would not be acquired outside the school?

The identification of the specific goals of the schools has been a continuing battleground. The Committee of Ten, chaired by Harvard President Charles W. Eliot, suggested in 1893 that training the mind to solve problems was the goal, and that any group of difficult subjects would suffice if the study were continued long enough with a competent instructor. The classical high school curriculum of the time resulted, comprising large doses of Latin, Greek, higher mathematics, and the like. Important changes in educational philosophy, however, led to formation of a new statement in 1918 by the NEA's Committee on the Reorganization of Secondary Education; their "Seven Cardinal Principles" were: health, command of the fundamental processes, worthy home membership, vocation, civic education, worthy use of leisure, and ethical character.[2]

More recent attempts to identify educational goals have served principally to clarify and extend the Seven Cardinal Principles. Among these was *Purposes of Education in American Democracy*, produced by the Educational Policies Committee in 1938.[3] Here the objectives were written in behavioral terms and classified within four areas:

The Objectives of Self-Realization
The Objectives of Human Relationship
The Objectives of Economic Efficiency
The Objectives of Civic Responsibility

A massive, long-term project is presently underway in the National Assessment of Educational Progress. It began in 1964 with support from the Carnegie Corporation and Ford Foundation. More recent grants have come from the U.S. Office of Education. Its leadership includes some of the most respected names in educational philosophy and evaluation. The curriculum was divided into areas, objectives were identified, evaluative procedures developed, and assessment has begun on selected populations on the following schedule:

1969–70	Science; Writing; Citizenship
1970–71	Reading; Literature
1971–72	Music; Social Studies
1972–73	Mathematics; Science, Career and Occupational Development
1973–74	Reading; Writing
1974–75	Citizenship; Art
1975–76	Mathematics; Science
1976–77	Reading; Literature
1977–78	Music; Social Studies
1978–79	Mathematics, Science; Career and Occupational Development
1979–80	Reading, Writing
1980–81	Citizenship; Art

---

[2] Washington, D.C.: U.S. Bureau of Education, 1918, republished by the Office of Education, U.S. Department of Health, Education and Welfare, 1962.

[3] Washington, D.C.: National Education Association.

It will be noted that each of the ten areas is scheduled for one or more re-assessments and since only part of the exercises will be reported, the unreported ones can be re-used and comparisons made at the time of each re-assessment.

Having participated in the early construction of exercises in music, this author believes that the project is essentially valid and should have a significant effect upon the goals and procedures of schooling. This being the case, the objectives of the music assessment are summarized below as an aid in defining the task of administration in music education.[4]

I. Perform a piece of music.
> A. Sing (technical proficiency not required).
> B. Play or sing (technical proficiency required).
> C. Invent and improvise (technical proficiency not required).

II. Read standard musical notation.
> A. Identify the elements of notation, such as clefs, letter names of notes, duration symbols, key signatures, and dynamic markings.
> B. Identify the correct notation for familiar pieces.
> C. Follow notation while listening to music.
> D. Sight-sing.

III. Listen to music with understanding.
> A. Perceive the various elements of music, such as timbre, rhythm, melody and harmony, and texture.
> B. Perceive structure in music.
> C. Distinguish some differing types and functions of music.
> D. Be aware of (and recognize) some features of historical styles in music.

IV. Be knowledgeable about some musical instruments, some of the terminology of music, methods of performance and forms, some of the standard literature of music, and some aspects of the history of music.
> A. Know the meanings of common musical terms used in connection with the performance of music, and identify musical instruments and performing ensembles in illustrations.
> B. Know standard pieces of music by title, or composer, or brief descriptions of music, or of literary-pictorial materials associated with the music from its inception.

---

[4] Available through National Assessment Information Services, 300 Lincoln Tower, 1860 Lincoln Street, Denver, Colorado, 80203.

C. Know prominent composers and performers by name and chief accomplishment.
D. Know something of the history of music.

V. Know about the musical resources of the community and seek musical experiences by performing music.
    A. Know whether or not there are music libraries and stores in the community, and know where concerts are given.
    B. Seek to perform music by playing, singing, taking lessons, joining performing groups, etc.

VI. Make judgments about music, and value the personal worth of music.
    A. Distinguish parodies from their models.
    B. Be able to describe an important personal "musical" experience.

As far as music education goes, the National Assessment program tends to confirm music's place as one of the primary areas of the curriculum of general education, expected of all citizens, and should materially assist in the effort to include the subject as a requirement for college entrance. Secondly, it takes us further along the road toward a detailed prescription of specific musical behaviors to be achieved, and in the direction of more adequate evaluative procedure. Finally, the results of the assessment should provide some evidence of the strengths and weaknesses of past and current efforts in music education and thus establish a springboard for curriculum improvement. This will not only affect the elementary and secondary school music programs, but will also have strong implications for change in the professional programs in higher education—for the preparation of music teachers, scholars, composers, and performing artists.

Without awaiting the results of the assessment, however, it should be immediately apparent to the reader that there is vast inconsistency between these stated competencies and the actual competencies now promoted by the schools and produced in their graduates. In the first place, the youth of America seem to maintain a familiarity with the current styles of popular music through purchase of recordings and listening to performances of well-known popular artists via radio, television, and local appearances. But very few can demonstrate any technical understanding of what they are hearing, nor can many read musical notation with ease. Some have learned by rote to sing a number of these songs, but the quality of performance is often barely admissible. Some ten million own guitars, but most of these have merely acquired the skill to fake a few basic harmonic progressions. Knowledge and understanding of musical history and style is only rudimentary in the vast majority of cases; their aesthetic judgment lacks the foundation of acquaintance with any significant body of literature from our vast musical heritage.

The simple fact is that most citizens react at a very low level of musical sensibility. They respond to rhythm and melody and dynamic contrast, as they are born to do. They like familiar tunes, especially those without great structural complexity. They often like to be surrounded by musical sound because it is distracting. But most do not often choose to attend formal concerts, unless they must transport their own children. Paradoxically, music occupies a big place in our lives, but largely on a natural, automatic basis; few individuals show the results of skillful training in the higher aspects of the art and these mostly comprise those who have explored the art as a vocation.

This result is attributed largely to the fact that the schools have said one thing and done another. They have spoken of broad and general musical training in the elementary schools and have mainly taught rote songs—often not using even good folk material. Even this much instruction has often been shallow because the classroom teacher couldn't or wouldn't teach it, and the necessary music specialist didn't exist. Music teachers have spoken of the right of every child to music and have then limited beginning instrumental instruction to those who had a certain test score or grade average and whose parents could provide them an instrument. Band directors have talked much about developing their players' musicianship and have then drilled them feverishly on marching evolutions while playing simple show tunes as loudly as possible.

Significantly, administrative direction is often held responsible for this state of affairs, supposedly catering to use of music at athletic functions and general promotional use at the expense of valid musical outcomes.

On the other hand, one may occasionally observe a school where, without a great deal of fanfare, most of the students are profitably involved with music. Music is studied daily, with purpose, in the elementary classrooms and in the junior high school, and there are large bands, orchestras, and choral groups in the high school. A number of small ensembles also rehearse regularly and, whenever musical activity is observed, there is exhibited interest and good will and the literature used is worthwhile and performed expressively.

In such schools, administrative personnel are invariably proud of the music program and show obvious intention to support and maintain it in every way possible. Whether favorable administrative attitude is a cause or a result, it is manifestly necessary to the continued existence of any flourishing school music program. Perhaps the fundamental characteristic of school administration is that it develops certain basic assumptions regarding the purposes of education and how to secure them, and then sets about producing the means to achieve those ends. As part of that format, the quality and status of the music program is of the greatest importance.

TYPES AND LEVELS OF SCHOOLING

Our concern is with the administration of music programs in every type and level of educational institution. Music instruction does indeed occur in a variety of school settings, and these differences are bound to affect the administrative operation.

THE PUBLIC SCHOOLS

The American public schools, grades K–12, constitute the most prevalent and characteristic wing of our system of education. They developed mainly during the nineteenth century, in response to this nation's strong intention to produce literate, informed citizens, capable of self-government and economic self-sufficiency. It has been regarded as the responsibility of each state to provide and maintain public schools. Through the state constitutions and legislative enactment, the school districts have been defined, monies have been provided, and regulations have been developed for the certification of teachers.

By the early 1930s, there were approximately 127,000 school districts. Then a rapid trend set in for consolidation, so that by 1968 this number was reduced to 20,000; the average area was 150 square miles, with a population of 10,500, and an enrollment of 2,100. But a good many of these were still one-room rural schools; at the same time, 150 city school districts enrolled 12,000,000 pupils—about 30% of the nation's total—and employed over 25% of the nation's teachers.[5]

The use of busing tends to produce further consolidation, which is generally considered more efficient and educationally sound, although the size of school populations in urban centers has become a special problem. There, the thought is to create subdistricts which are more manageable.

Each school district is governed by a local board, usually elected by the citizens. Functioning under state regulation, each school board meets regularly to hear, discuss, and act on all matters affecting the local schools.

The school system includes all the teachers and students and physi-

---

[5] Calvin Grieder, Thurman M. Pierce, and K. Forbes Jordan, *Public School Administration*, 3rd ed. (New York: The Ronald Press Co., 1969), pp. 8–9.

cal properties within control of one board of education. Within the local school systems, various patterns of organization exist. The National Education Association estimated in 1966 that the following percentages prevailed among 12,130 local districts enrolling more than 300 pupils.[6]

6-3-3	21.5%
6-6	22.4
6-2-4	11.9
8-4	21.4
7-5	3.4
others (6-3-3-2, 6-2-4-2, 5-3-4, 7-2-3, 4-4-4, etc.)	19.4
	100.0%

The 8-4 or 6-2-4 plan is largely a survivor of the days when most citizens completed eight grades in the "common school," and many did not proceed to high school. Thus, high school districts were organized to collect graduates from two or more elementary school districts. There are still today many county high schools, consolidated high schools, etc., organized separately from the elementary school systems within the same geographic areas. Lack of administrative continuity in these situations is not conducive to healthy music programs.

Even with unified elementary and secondary school districts, the general practice has been to spread several elementary schools (K–6) widely throughout the community, which feed their graduates into larger and more centralized junior high and senior high school buildings. Enrollments of 175–700—with one to four classrooms per grade—have been considered standard for elementary school buildings. Three-quarters of a mile has been considered the standard radius for walking students in the elementary schools, and secondary students were formerly expected to walk further or to secure rides. But the busing of rural students has expanded to include urban students, and the practice has increased with recent attempts to effect racial balance and to override housing discrimination. In many communities, each existing elementary school building has been converted into a center for a particular grade level, so that all children in that grade are transported there for school and a complete racial mix is achieved.

If this trend continues, the neighborhood school will gradually become extinct. It will be much more efficient to develop "school parks,"

---

[6] NEA Research Division, "Public School Programs and Practices," *Research Bulletin 45* (December, 1967).

where all grades from nursery school through senior high school and perhaps junior college will be placed in one central location. This will promote lower land and building costs, simpler transportation schedules, more efficient employment of teachers, more flexible grouping of students, and improved scheduling of special classes and activities.

Advocates of the neighborhood school have reacted strongly, however, against court-ordered busing to effect racial balance. The problem strikes at deeply held convictions and has become a potent political issue. Pending a final outcome of this debate, the movement toward more centralized schooling may well be slowed or stopped.

The relative size of a school system and the contiguity of instructional facilities has a big effect upon the administration of the music program—since these factors relate to the assignment of instructional tasks, the grouping of students, and the flexibility of scheduling. Concentration of educational activity is normally helpful to the music program.

In any case, the mixed organizational structure of the American schools results in a great variety of administrative patterns and combinations within school music programs. The very small school, of course, may have only a part-time music teacher—one or two at most—and the chief responsibility is to secure effective general music instruction in the elementary classrooms and to develop all-school choral and instrumental organizations. The administrative function in music is necessarily superimposed upon these responsibilities. Larger school systems allow more specialized assignments, and music programs in very large urban centers are staffed by a number of special music teachers, consultants, and administrative personnel, each responsible for a limited sector of the entire program.

Non-public Elementary and Secondary Schools

There are a number of school systems operated outside the state-controlled schools. These include the parochial schools, university laboratory schools, privately operated academies, commercial music schools, and the like. The actual number of such institutions is difficult to determine, since they are often small and transitory, but it is estimated that around ten percent of the school population is enrolled in them. They exist because a certain proportion of families desire to emphasize certain religious, moral, economic or social class values which they feel the public schools do not provide. Since, however, these schools must be financed largely by these same families, as a burden superimposed upon the taxes already paid for support of the public schools, facilities are often substandard. In many cases, this fact is alleviated by the use of non-salaried instructors available in some parochial institutions.

The organization and administration of these non-public schools is similar to the public schools. The differences in philosophy, in clientele, and in the source of funds, however, tend to produce somewhat different approaches. Music programs, for example, often seem to stress academic and disciplinary values, yet with strong overtones of "public relations"; in other instances, as in the case of many university laboratory schools, experimental and highly specialized forms of music instruction are frequently found.

PRE-SCHOOL EDUCATION

Kindergartens are a longstanding institution in the United States, yet are not universally available. Many are offered on a tuition basis. Nursery schools for three- and four-year-olds have operated only in the private sector until quite recently. Now, with the increasing awareness of the crucial importance of early childhood education, there is a trend toward the inclusion of two and three years of pre-schooling leading to first grade. Participation is normally on a voluntary, not compulsory, basis, and sessions are typically for one-half days. Music tends to be a prominent feature in these pre-school classes.

INSTITUTIONS OF HIGHER LEARNING

The World Almanac of 1970 lists about fifteen hundred four-year colleges and universities, of which some four hundred are state supported. A number of these also offer graduate work leading to master and doctoral degrees. In addition, there are numerous junior colleges or community colleges which offer two-year diplomas and preparation for transfer to senior colleges; this category of institution is expanding so rapidly that any statistical reference may be misleading.

Most of these institutions of higher education offer some form of musical training and some 14,500 faculty members are listed in the *1970–72 Directory of Music Faculties in Colleges and Universities in America*.[7] Nearly four hundred of the larger and more professional schools and departments of music have joined together within the National Association of Schools of Music, which has been a major force

---

[7] The College Music Society, Harry B. Lincoln, ed., State University of New York, Binghamton, 1970.

in accreditation and in administrative operation since its founding in 1924.

As would be expected, the size of these music units varies from groupings of two and three faculty members who handle all the basic musical activities, to bodies of a thousand and more music students served by several hundred music instructors. In most cases, these music departments feature specialized instruction toward professional goals and thus require centralized administration. Later sections of this book will deal in some detail with problems in this area.

CONCEPTS OF EDUCATIONAL ADMINISTRATION

The administrative function is an inherent force in any organization. It has been equated with "management" and has been defined as the means by which one promotes the goals of an organization through the utilization of existing structures and procedures. "Leadership," on the other hand, has been defined as the development of *new* procedures and structures.[8] It is not an exclusive property of administrative officials.

In other words, the administrative officers are usually identified as "the establishment," working through channels and acting on procedures created by law and precedent. Forces for change in these patterns are just as likely to come from other individuals both within and outside the organization (i.e., other faculty members, students, and parents), who discern the necessity for new approaches.

Prevalent administrative structure is the product of long evolution. In actual fact, school administration was originally accomplished by the headmaster or building principal, who was often the school's founder or proprietor, and who was generally supported in his duties by a committee of citizens.

Formal school organization borrowed much from industrial management. Frederic Taylor, foreman at the Midvale Steel Company in Philadelphia, concentrated upon motion analysis and standardization of tools; the term "scientific management" was coined to fit his procedures. Henri Fayol concentrated upon broader aspects of administration and emphasized personnel control. Luther Gulick outlined the task in seven phases: Planning, Organizing, Staffing, Directing, Coordinating, Reporting, and Budgeting. Further contributions to administrative theory were made by Mary Parker Follett, who dealt with the delegation of authority,

---

8 James H. Lipham, "Leadership and Administration," in *Behavioral Science and Educational Administration,* ed. Daniel Griffiths (Chicago: National Society for the Study of Education, 1964) pp. 119–41.

Chester Barnard, who emphasized creative cooperation, and Herbert Simon, who questioned the application of "scientific management" to human beings.

The theory of school administration was developed around these principles during the early years of this century. The emphasis was upon the business details of school administration. But a much broader concept was introduced after the Second World War with the work of Paul Mort, John K. Norton, Daniel E. Griffiths, and others. School administration now tends to be conceived largely as an exercise in judgment, mainly directed at decision-making. It should be noted, however, that the chief executive is not expected to make the decisions personally, but to monitor the decision-making process. All other aspects of the task— i.e., planning, organizing, communicating, influencing, coordinating, evaluating—are seen as preliminary and consequential to the making of useful decisions.

Of course, students of educational administration *per se* are thinking largely of the roles played by superintendents and principals in their relations with school boards, teachers, and students. Most readers of this book, on the other hand, will tend to view these matters from the standpoint of music supervisors, music department chairmen, and directors of school performing groups, as they deal with other school officials and with other music teachers and their students. Our point of reference is always "normal practice" in music programs as they exist in the elementary and secondary schools and colleges of the United States.

THE QUALITIES OF SUCCESSFUL ADMINISTRATION

Before turning to specific administrative roles affecting the music program and the tasks to be accomplished, which will be treated in subsequent chapters, it will be useful to discuss broad principles which should guide the administrator. An excellent outline of these is given by Morphet, Johns, and Reller:[9]

The effectiveness of an organization is enhanced

1. by having a single executive head.
2. by clear definition of goals and purposes.
3. when every person in the organization knows to whom and for what he is responsible.
4. when superordinates delegate authority to subordinates.

---

[9] Edgar L. Morphet, Roe L. Johns, and Theodore L. Reller, *Educational Organization and Administration: Concepts, Practices, and Issues,* 2nd ed. (Englewood Cliffs, N.J.: Prentice-Hall, Inc., 1967), pp. 94–98.

5. by the division of labor and task specialization.

6. by the development of standardized procedures for routine administrative operation.

7. by assigning each administrator no greater number of persons than he can directly supervise.

8. by continuing policies and programs until results can be evaluated.

9. when it makes provision for innovation and change.

10. when the organization provides security for its members.

11. by personnel policies which include selecting the competent, training the inexperienced, eliminating the incompetent, and providing incentives for all members of the organization.

12. when provision is made not only for evaluating the products of the organization but also the organization itself.

The above principles underline the primacy of personnel relationships. School administration deals with personnel in three dimensions—with professional colleagues, with students, and with the public who are concerned with the schools. In terms of the faculty and staff, the administrator is constantly employed in defining the tasks to be accomplished and in finding the best people to do them. Then, he must get to know these individuals, their strengths and weaknesses, and discover how to deal with each one so as to secure his best efforts. He will find that one responds well to constructive suggestions but that another needs mostly praise. Some people, too, need limited assignments while others will do better with extra tasks which tap their surplus energies and make them feel more "involved." Each faculty member will require special handling. An "open door policy" is advisable.

Faculty members tend to identify with particular subgroups or cliques, and they often become unreasonably partisan. Administrators generally need to attempt to reduce these barriers to good teamwork. The first requisite, of course, is not to become specifically identified with any one of these groups. The administrator will do well not to criticize his colleagues behind their backs, and to stress instead their positive contributions.

Try as he may, however, the administrator is due for criticism. He is in the position of the man in Aesop's fable who was criticized alike for leading the donkey, letting his son ride, riding alone and then together with his son, and finally carrying the donkey. Whenever things are not going smoothly, it is easy to blame the administrator. The answer, of course, is efficiency in anticipating and meeting problems when possible, and the good humor and patience to put up with the blame when things go wrong. The administrator simply cannot allow himself

to brood over the direct and implied criticisms which come his way. Neither must he allow these to color his objective judgment of the over-all effectiveness of those who make them.

One of the most difficult situations with professional personnel occurs when a faculty member was not properly selected, and it is found that he does not grow, does not measure up to his responsibilities, or has a divisive influence. When all reasonable corrective measures have failed, the administrator must face the possibility that it will be better for the organization if the individual is removed from his post, or encouraged to seek another position. The problem is greatly compounded when tenure has already been achieved.

Another measure of effective administration is in the establishment of proper relations with students. In a basic sense, of course, they are the raw material of the schools, and their development constitutes the end product. In another sense they are colleagues in the educational enterprise. Administration must always hold their true welfare as the main criterion in the determination of educational policy. If anything useful is to be accomplished, good student attitudes and morale must be maintained, and purposeful communication with the administration is one means to that end. But students are transients; tested procedures should not be altered simply at the whim of a few students who think that they have invented new remedies. Flexibility in dealing with students is a good rule.

Administrative tactics must also respond effectively to the expectations of parents and other citizens interested in the school program. Their opinions are likely to be conflicting, with one wing interested in promoting experimentation and various forms of enrichment, while others will support traditionalism, retrenchment, and orderly procedure. The school music program is especially vulnerable to these forces since it is so often on public display. The effort must be to stress educational outcomes rather than promotional values.

A second large sector of administrative concern lies in educational logistics. Buildings must be planned and built, custodial services arranged, budgets created, equipment purchased and stored, classes and rehearsals scheduled, concert dates held and publicized, scholarships awarded, curricular requirements established and enforced, student counseling and advisement conducted, instructional supplies distributed, inquiries answered, payrolls met, and so on. One major part of successful administration, then, is simply serving as a clearinghouse to expedite the multitude of detail which surrounds instruction. Much good planning is necessary, along with sensible delegation of tasks. Provision for effective secretarial service, counseling, and business management are a necessity.

But the administrator himself must keep "on top of the job" and not allow correspondence to languish on his desk unanswered. At all costs, his office must never become a bottleneck.

The third major ingredient of successful administration is providing direction to the organization, and this is largely accomplished in terms of decision-making. In fact, the administrative hierarchy is fundamentally based upon each individual's nearness to the point of ultimate decision. Big decisions are made at the top and lesser decisions further down the ladder. But in school circles, effective input from all levels is considered highly desirable when important decisions are to be made. This contributes to better execution of tasks. Thus it is that various committees of faculty and students are established to deal with educational policy, curriculum, faculty welfare, student admission, scholarships, etc. The local PTA is in a sense a large laymen's committee on the conduct of the schools. Likewise with the Band Parents' Club. All of these groups are, in fact, advisory to the administrator, but he is wise who gives his committees full scope and information and then incorporates their recommendations into the operational format of the school program.

It is difficult to say just how much authority and responsibility should be shared with the faculty, students, and interested laymen. Ideally, the ultimate responsibility for the *conduct* of affairs lies with the administrative officials, *guided* by the expressed concerns of their constituents. But the administrator makes the final decision after weighing all factors and opinions and then choosing the option which will tend to further the most balanced and effective educational program for all the students. In the process, if the administration wishes to avoid usurpation of its powers, it must anticipate needs, provide objectives, and suggest solutions. It must finally act openly and decisively and respond rationally to any criticism.

QUESTIONS FOR DISCUSSION

1. What is the relationship between the purposes of a school and the administrative task?
2. What criteria are used in determining the content of schooling? What facets of musical study are justifiable under those criteria?
3. Are the objectives of the National Assessment in music feasible for individual local school systems? Do they relate in any way to collegiate music programs?
4. Describe trends in school organization. Contrast the roles of

public and privately controlled institutions. How do these factors affect patterns for handling music instruction?

5. How has the theory of educational administration borrowed from industrial management? What is the inherent function of school administration? Who participates in this task?

6. How does administration relate to faculty? What principles must guide the administration in dealing with students and the public?

7. What are the essential administrative responsibilities in terms of organization of the school and its music program and in providing the necessary facilities? How and to what extent are these responsibilities shared?

SUGGESTED READINGS

Franklin, Marian Pope, ed., *School Organization: Theory and Practice.* Chicago: Rand McNally and Co., 1967.

Grieder, Calvin, Truman M. Pierce, and K. Forbes Jordan, *Public School Administration,* 3rd ed. New York: The Ronald Press Co., 1969.

Morphet, Edgar L., Roe L. Johns, and Theodore L. Reller, *Educational Organization and Administration,* 2nd ed. Englewood Cliffs, N.J.: Prentice-Hall, Inc., 1967, chaps. 1–7.

National Society for the Study of Education, *The Changing American School.* Sixty-fifth Yearbook, Part II. Chicago: University of Chicago Press, 1966.

CHAPTER TWO

administrative roles and the music program

Except in the case of independent music schools and conservatories, music programs exist as integral units within large institutional structures. Within these patterns, as we have pointed out, the size of a school system and the level of instruction have much to do with defining actual administrative roles. Titles alone do not provide a reliable index of real function. A brief discussion of the essential school services will help to make this distinction.

ADMINISTRATION, SUPERVISION, AND INSTRUCTION

Instruction, or teaching, is the primary function of the school. It involves all direct efforts to secure useful learning on the part of the students. In brief, the teacher must determine the behaviors he is seeking and the kinds of experience that pertain to them. Then, after assessing the present background of his students, he engages them in those learning activities which—with the proper information and his insightful presentation—will heighten student perception and stimulate useful responses. In short, the environment is produced which modifies behavior toward the objectives of the teacher and the school. This is what music teachers are doing in the classroom and in rehearsal.

Administration, as we have said, is aimed at facilitating this teaching process; it provides the means of instruction, including not only the buildings and equipment but also the teachers and their offerings, and establishes the fiscal and organizational machinery to make this come off. Its method is managerial.

Supervision is dedicated to the improvement of instruction. The real music supervisor is an administrator of a special kind—a staff officer rather than an executive officer—who works directly with teachers and students in planning the course of study, demonstrating better materials and techniques, and aiding the teachers and promoting their music program in every way possible.

Relatively few individuals in music education succeed for very long in confining their duties to any one of these realms—instruction, administration, or supervision. Regardless of title, many are involved in all three in varying proportion.

The title of music supervisor, for example, has long been held in great vogue. Since it implies some sort of leadership and special responsibility, young music educators tend to seek the position. Indeed, if there are only two music teachers in a school system, one is sure to be titled supervisor of instrumental music and the other will be vocal music supervisor. Some years ago, indeed, college programs for the preparation of music educators were commonly labeled "Instrumental Music Supervisors' Curriculum" and "Vocal Music Supervisors' Curriculum," and the national organization for music educators was the Music Supervisors National Conference.

As populations have increased and school districts have consolidated, the job of music supervisor has tended to become more specialized. But many still wear three hats. Only in very large school systems does their role become primarily managerial rather than supervisory.

The same phenomenon of overlapping functions is often observed with other school officials, especially in the case of principals, who usually handle certain supervisory functions within their buildings as well as administrative services. In trying to differentiate between these functions, other titles have come into use, such as Coordinator of Curriculum Services, who heads the supervisory team, Director of Music, which implies concentration upon the administrative function, and Music Consultant, which connotes more purely supervisory activities.

THE MANAGEMENT PROCESS

In order to reduce the confusion resulting from the indiscriminate use of titles and overlapping duties, it is helpful to consider the general management process and its organizational features, as defined by the academic discipline of business management.

Administration is a managerial process. The job is to secure the objectives of the organization through effective planning, organization, and control. In the case of an educational institution, the inherent primary objective is the production of properly educated youth. The functional relationships of personnel are therefore determined by the part they must play in the educative effort.

There are two basic roles in an organization—operative and administrative. The operative in this case is the teacher who is entrusted with the direct production of educational values through instruction of the students. Where there are numbers of teachers working together in a school, it then becomes necessary to produce a cohesive, organized attack, by means of three managerial functions—planning, organizing, and controlling. The individual teacher, of course, plans, organizes, and controls his own activity, but the administrator must assume responsibility for *coordinative* planning, organization, and control of the group effort.

PLANNING

It is obvious that whatever the school seeks to achieve needs to be preceded by adequate planning. It is the process by which uncertainty is avoided and change may be anticipated. It also helps to focus attention upon the objectives of the group and tends toward maximum efficiency and economy. Finally, it provides the basis for proper control of operations. In short, it is the method by which one puts the odds of success in his favor. It is an inherent responsibility of administration to see that this function is properly accomplished.

Planning is inherently a mental process, involving reference to the unit's objectives, establishment of situational premises, outlining alternate plans and choosing the best, establishing a practical sequence and timing, communicating with concerned parties, and providing for reports and other checks on results. It may be seen that good planning requires some intelligence and constant reference to past experience and the needs of the particular situation. And it is true that the plans of one segment of an organization often clash with those of another. Only top management is in a position to discern the entire relationship of the parts to the whole. Each administrator is responsible, therefore, to see that planning within his sector of control is adequately coordinated so that the best possible results will obtain. Each project must be carefully adjusted to ongoing operations so that total efficiency is not sacrificed. Thus it is that the yearly calendar of musical events needs to be planned as a unit, so that major events are well separated to minimize conflicts for performing personnel, equipment, and publicity. Likewise, music class schedules need to be carefully adjusted to the availability of the auditorium and practice field, which spaces are also in demand by other activities. It should also be recognized that longer-range planning is required at the higher administrative levels. The university president or school superintendent is accustomed to planning ten and twenty years in advance his moves toward expansion of the campus and faculty and programs, in keeping with his appraisal of the potential enrollment of his institution. At the same time, the music executive needs to be planning several years ahead for added housing and equipment in terms of the growth which he can reasonably project. Planning for beginning instrumental classes and for the acquisition of musical instruments must take place several years in advance if the band and orchestra director is to achieve his balanced performing organization. And planning must begin several months prior to any successful production of a football half time show, musical, or concert.

Planning must always remain flexible, in order to take proper account of other people and the need for their adequate cooperation. Otherwise, an inflexible administrator will discover that his plans are ignored. He must delegate much of the detail in making plans and executing them. For this reason, many rely upon committee planning. This offers the opportunity for group deliberation and judgment and tends toward wider communication. It may help to achieve better execution of plans through better understanding and acceptance. But committees are costly of time and money and they are subject to compromise or domination. It is necessary to select the members with care and to give them well-defined authority and scope. It must be understood that the committee serves a staff function and so its recommendations are just that—proposals that are subject to adoption, amendment, or rejection by the individual or body that instituted the committee.

A major aspect of long-term planning is *policy-making*. The idea is to facilitate decision-making by establishing a basis for handling recurring problems. A policy supplies the needed relationship between the organization's objectives and the kinds of actions it will take to fulfill them. Once established, it extends the control of the administrator without his immediate participation in the situation, by indicating what direction he would take. Ideally, it:

1. discourages deviations from planned actions.
2. promotes consistent action.
3. promotes intelligent cooperation.
4. facilitates coordination of action.

5. fosters initiative at lower levels.
6. guides equitable personnel relations.
7. provides a basis for determining quality of executive action.
8. guides future planning.

A familiar problem in university schools of music, for example, lies in the realm of scholarships. A policy is needed, and the following statement is typical:

> The objectives of the music school depend greatly upon securing those students most talented and likely to succeed, regardless of their financial situation. Available scholarships, therefore, should go to those who evidence most financial need and, among those, to those who demonstrate the most talent and motivation. The committee will consult each student's Request for Financial Assistance, his teachers' recommendations and his grade average, as well as his audition ranking, in making recommendations for the awards.

It should be noted that such a formulation is in two parts—stating both the governing principle and the application. It provides a rule for action. Yet it is flexible and gives the committee needed latitude. Similar policies are needed for all realms where the need for decision will recur. Formulation needs to be followed by dissemination, education and acceptance and possible amendment, application, and control.

ORGANIZING

Another facet of management is organization toward the achievement of its goals. Organizing is the process of establishing relationships among the personnel, physical factors, and functions to the end that all are related and combined into an effective goal-directed unit. Project organization is a relatively clear-cut concept that can be illustrated in terms of the task force assembled to plan and produce an opera. But structural organization is a complex topic that defines all administrative operation and must be explained in some detail.

The first point which must be considered is the *line and staff concept*. It is based upon the natural functions of the organization and, in terms of an educational institution, these usually include instruction, business and finance, physical plant, transportation, library service, food service, medical service, research, student advisement and counseling, recreation, area service, and public relations. It may be noted that instruction is placed first, because this is the function relating most directly to the primary objective of the institution. The teachers are therefore the operatives, and these are divided into subject areas or grade levels and placed in the charge of appropriate department heads or principals. Related units are then grouped and assigned to higher officers such as deans, vice-presidents, or assistant superintendents, who all work at the direction of the chief executive—the president or superintendent—who is in turn supported by a board representing the public or other special constituency. This organization represents *the line.*

The line concept derives from military usage, where "line officers" are placed in charge of fighting units and report directly to their superiors. "Staff officers," on the other hand, are appointed to act in an advisory or technical capacity to their chiefs, and are assigned specific tasks; they work with their counterparts at other levels but do not exercise direct command of the troops. This pattern is roughly outlined below:

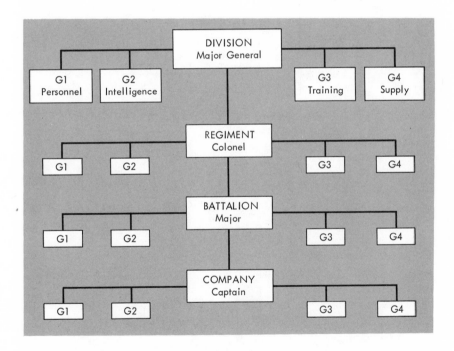

The staff officers are asked advice and give it, but any plan that is adopted must be activated only upon orders given the troops through the commanding officer. He is held responsible and accountable for the decision.

Similarly, in an educational institution, the chain of command is from the chief executive officer, through the vice presidents or assistant

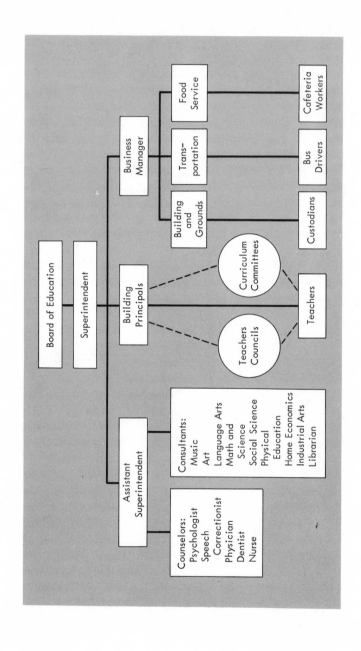

superintendents and their deans or principals, and to the teachers and their students. The other functions of the institution—finance, plant, transportation, and all other special services—are secondary and are the responsibility of staff officers. These individuals have line authority over their own sub-organizations, but do not properly hold direct authority over the teachers and students. A basic outline for such organization is given on page 26.

In this instance, it will be noted that the music consultant is separated from his colleagues in music by reason of their primary responsibility to the principal. In actual practice, of course, music specialists tend to identify with one another and to look for leadership from within their own ranks. This fact can lead to a finer music program, so long as essential lines of authority are not bypassed.

Departmental organization is generally more clear-cut at the university level, where a music program of any size will be placed within a larger school or college. The executive head of the music unit thus reports to the head of his College of Fine Arts, who in turn is supervised by an academic Dean or Vice-President. The typical organization chart is as follows.

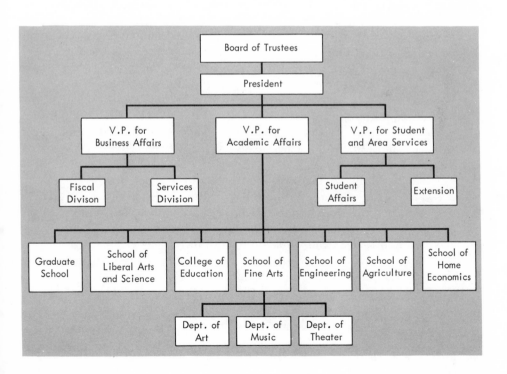

The development of such organization comes by a natural process of growth and accretion. For illustration, we may use the example of a former one-room school, many thousands of which once existed in thinly populated rural areas. At our one-room school, the schoolmaster served as instructor of all his students in all the basic subjects, and also functioned as his own student counselor, purchasing agent, accountant, buildings and groundskeeper. But through the years, as more people moved into the district and more children were born, as more students went to school and stayed longer, and with pressure to consolidate with surrounding districts for more efficient operation, it became necessary and desirable to acquire a larger plant and to enlarge the faculty. As these added faculty members were acquired, division of labor occurred, so that each was assigned to teach certain grade levels or subjects and one was designated to direct the operation as principal. As time went on, the principal's span of control became too large, so that a superintendent was appointed and one individual was assigned as principal of the elementary grades and another for the secondary level. This basic administrative line structure had to be supplemented by staff positions in the form of a superintendent of buildings and grounds, a business manager, a cafeteria manager, and a director of transportation. Finally, it became convenient to designate department heads for the various subjects and to secure supervisors to advise and assist the various classroom teachers. The process continued until the school organization reached the stage represented by our previous diagram. Educational institutions may be observed in all stages of growth with corresponding differences in structural organization.

As educational institutions develop, then, it is clear that administrative structure evolves into several levels, and the proper delegation of authority and responsibility becomes critical to the effective conduct of affairs.

Responsibility is the obligation to perform a task to the best of one's ability according to direction. It is defined in terms of the position title and the stated expectations when one is appointed and accepts the position. It is true of course that conditions change and reorganization may occur so that an individual's responsibilities may require redefinition; nevertheless, it is a serious duty of every administrator to outline clearly the scope of the job to be accomplished by each of his appointees. Failure to do this leads to "empire building," where an individual has indefinite limits to his job and thus tends to expand it to the limits of his capability, becoming "the indispensable man."

This raises the issue of the administrator's responsibility not only for his own performance, but for the activities of those in his unit. The classical position is that he is so responsible, but it is not really true that anyone can guarantee perfection in those he appointed or inherited. Nor can he be held morally responsible for their mistakes and shortcomings. As an administrator, he is responsible for his *own* poor planning, poor delegation, poor control, etc., but not for unforeseen character flaws in his subordinates which might produce severe consequences. Instead, he is *accountable;* that is, he is expected to have an accurate explanation of any shortcomings which may occur. Each administrator is held accountable for his own sphere of operations, including those of his direct subordinates.

Accountability is best established by regular and special reports to one's superior, outlining the problems that are being faced, the actions planned, and the results of previous actions. This process allows judgment of one's accomplishment based upon realistic understanding of the situation and the actual resources at one's command. It is often found that one is being expected to accomplish things that are beyond his powers. For example, a band director may have been hired and told that he is responsible to build a fine marching band, which he does not produce. He is accountable for this, but since his reasonable requests for the necessary rehearsal time and equipment were not honored, his explanation must be accepted that he is not entirely responsible for the result.

Administrative authority is another concept which is often misunderstood. Authority consists of the *right* to perform assigned functions in order to make possible a satisfactory accomplishment of job objectives. This right is delegated by society to the governing board of the educational institution, and to each administrative level in turn, as necessary to meet its responsibilities.

According to this principle, since an administrator must delegate authority to his subordinates, he is usually given the right to control their appointment. However, there is an opposing theory, based upon the idea that one can only exercise authority effectively to the limits of acceptance of those who must work with him. This allows for the natural emergence of informal leadership and, in this sense, delegation of authority comes from below. This theory is the basis for faculty election of school officials.

It is our strong belief, however, that the schools and colleges are agents of society, and not the creatures of the school personnel themselves—and, hence, authority and appointment must be from above. If, then, the individual administrator does not secure an effective working relationship with his subordinates and is unable to function adequately, it becomes necessary for higher authority to remove him from the post. In this way, the lower echelons of an organization retain an implied veto over administrative appointments.

The possibility of finding the wrong individual in a post arises because the *right* to act is not synonymous with the *power* to act—power being based upon actual possession of the resources and abilities needed for the particular job. For example, a very successful choral director may lack the essential ability to discharge the functions of a music department chairman. Sometimes these gaps in ability may be provided by staff officers who work with an individual administrator, but when this help is not forthcoming a serious breakdown will occur. Thus it is entirely possible for a top administrator who is weak in the realm of public relations to work effectively just so long as a strong public relations expert is working at his side.

There are two aspects of administrative authority—the right of decision and the right of command. The right to decide is essential to planning, while that of command is a necessity in directing and controlling the work of others. It is possible to withhold one or the other, saying in effect, "Tell them what I told you," or, "You decide how to do it." It is also possible to redelegate authority—along with the necessary resources and personnel for the job—and also to recall the delegation when the occasion no longer calls for it.

Delegation of authority and responsibility is made necessary by the limits of an administrator's *span of control.* Various estimates exist as to the optimum number of people one can effectively supervise. Depending upon the kind of operation and the quality of personnel, the general rule is that ten to thirty operatives may function well under one administrator, but from three to seven administrators and their units are usually considered to be the practical span of control for higher administrative posts. Since educational institutions may be said to contain largely expert personnel, requiring less intimate supervision, something near the higher figures may be expected to apply. Thus, twenty-five or thirty teachers may successfully be grouped together in a department and six or seven departments into a school or college. When these figures are exceeded, there are usually arrangements for subgrouping under assisting administrative personnel.

The increasing size of an organization is therefore one of the principal determinants of the need for delegation and its consequent, *decentralization.* Among the other factors tending toward decentralization are the complexity and specialized nature of the operation, physical dispersion, well-qualified and oriented personnel, and high morale. A move toward centralization is dictated by poor communications or crisis. Recent disturbances on American university campuses, for example, were invariably followed by moves toward the re-centralization of authority, as the students and their professors bypassed usual channels and went directly to the top for decisions. Shrinking budgets have caused a crisis in their turn, forcing arbitrary decisions from above as to the programs and personnel that shall be dropped.

CONTROL

The work of organizing an educational institution is comprehensive. It includes not only the acquisition of personnel and their organization into a functioning unit, but also the provision of physical plant and equipment, and the development of a properly balanced curriculum. More attention will be given to these items in later chapters. But plans and working facilities do not get the work done. They are applied by people working together under executive leadership. Control thus includes the direction and coordination of effort toward the planned educative results, along with a systematic check upon performance and the application of measures to minimize ineffective operation.

Administrative control is best conceived in terms of steps. Davis outlines these as follows:[1]

1. *Routine planning:* The authentication and publication of objectives, policies, plans, and programs.
2. *Scheduling:* The determination of deadlines for each phase of each program.
3. *Preparation:* The work of assuring that necessary financing will be completed, and that physical resources and personnel will be provided before a given phase of a program is scheduled to start. It has to do with assuring an adequate flow of resources and manpower to meet the requirements of the subordinate line and staff organizations over a period of time. It is not concerned directly with the specific requirements of individual projects.
4. *Dispatching:* The origination and release of orders activating a program, or some phase of it.
5. *Direction:* Conference between the administrative executive and his line and staff subordinates. It may include last-minute interpretations and explanations of general plans before or during the execution of a particular phase. It may lead to discussion of subsequent phases of a program that are about to be initiated.
6. *Supervision:* Review of the current status of the phase in process of execution with line and staff subordinates. This may be done individually or in conference, or both. It may be supported by field inspection trips.
7. *Comparison:* The receipt of administrative reports from subordinate line and staff divisions which evaluate the results of completed phases

---

[1] Ralph Currier Davis, *The Fundamentals of Top Management* (New York: Harper & Row, Publishers, 1951), p. 742.

by organizational groups. It includes the application of the Exception Principle in a consolidated, general administrative report for top management.

8. *Corrective action:* Conference between the principal administrative executive and his principal line and staff subordinates. It concerns the modification of general plans, policies, and programs that may be necessary to correct failures and to accomplish group objectives. It includes the activation of any administrative decisions that are reached.

A distinction should be made between *administrative control,* as outlined above, and *operational control.* Administrative control is a continuous process, exercised by the administrator as the several phases and subphases of his operation simultaneously unfold, each at its own rate of speed. New situations constantly arise and come under control as earlier programs mature and are phased out. Operative control, on the other hand, is the term used to describe the management of a single project which may be the delegated responsibility of a particular teacher. It may be illustrated in terms of the process involved in producing an opera. First comes *routine planning* of the project—assessing the qualities of the available singers and players and determining the particular work which they can best present. The general nature of the stage design and tech work will need to be established, the availability of musical scores and parts determined, costs estimated, and the auditorium reserved for rehearsals and performances. The next step is that of *scheduling,* or timing the execution of steps leading to the final dress rehearsal and performance. Here, it is of first importance to determine which phase of the operation will take longest to complete and to coordinate the other operations around it. In business circles this is called the "critical path." In our case, it is the selection and preparation of the singers who will do the difficult lead roles. Working backward from the performance date, a certain number of days must be calculated for the principals to prepare their singing and acting roles, which in turn determines the tryout date, the day that scores must be on hand for distribution, and the original deadline to order the scores. Similar timetables are established for training the chorus, preparing the orchestra, rehearsing the dancers, building costumes, designing and constructing sets, planning stage lighting, publicity campaign, program design and printing, ticket sales and ushers. *Preparation* is the critical step taken to assure that the needed factors are present when required. This involves determining the kind and amount of personnel and properties to be secured, finding them, and arranging for their attendance and delivery. *Dispatching* is the function of releasing authority to act to the lower echelons. At the proper time, in other words, those in charge of each phase of the operation are told to carry out their projects as planned. This is the point where one must look ahead to see that everything has been anticipated before final commitments are made. As the work begins, *direction* is exercised through interpreting, explaining, and instructing as needed to ensure correct execution of the tasks. The process of *supervision* is employed in overseeing the work, evaluating its progress, and redirecting it when damaging mistakes are being made. *Comparison* occurs during final rehearsals in the effort to discover weaknesses that would detract from the presentation. The final step, *corrective action,* consists in the removal of interferences and in making judicious readjustments which would lead to an improved performance on opening night.

ADMINISTRATIVE ROLES

Having discussed the nature of educational administration and its basis as defined by principles of management, it becomes practical to outline the various roles played by personnel in educational institutions as they relate to the music program. All educational institutions are characterized by an administrative structure, so that centralized authority is delegated in turn to lower echelons. Each will be discussed in turn.

FEDERAL AND STATE AGENCIES

American public schools have traditionally been locally operated and controlled, under the general authorization of their individual state governments. The U.S. Office of Education, however, as a part of the U.S. Department of Health, Education, and Welfare, has long provided the schools with information and research and has become increasingly involved with the disbursement and control of federal funds. There is a clear trend to continue in this direction, in view of pressures for equality of educational opportunity and the consequent moves to equalize financial aid to the schools. Consequently, the U.S. Office of Education steadily assumes more direct administrative influence over local school systems. The same is true of State Offices of Education and various State Superintendents of Public Instruction. Elected by the citizens, or appointed by others who have been elected by popular suffrage, they attempt to represent the generalized feelings and wishes of society regarding the content and conduct of public schooling. This is expressed in terms of regulations affecting local school board elections, tax rates, bond issues, fiscal procedure, certification of teachers, teaching contracts, minimum salaries, tenure and dismissal, compulsory student attendance, length of school year, and certain curriculum offerings. Periodic evaluative visits to schools are commonly made by state office personnel or their representatives. Most states now have state supervisors of music who attempt to aid the local music programs through promoting music clinics and university extension offerings, conferences, and published materials. Their area of administrative influence is significant.

Less organized structure is found in the case of private and church supported institutions and most colleges and universities, although there are voluntary associations of such institutions, as well as state and denominational boards of control which often exercise very direct supervision over finance and programs.

LOCAL GOVERNING BOARDS

Wide discretionary powers remain to local governing boards. Each local school board decides when and for what purpose bond issues shall be submitted. It receives and assigns state and federal funds. The members elect their own officers, call meetings, select a superintendent, and establish basic policy for their own school district. All appointments and payments are authorized and approved by the local school board.

By definition, local school board members are not professionals; their role is to represent the public interest. Hence, their main effort is not to administer the schools but to supervise that administration. This involves a considerable amount of study and discussion in order to develop and establish policy. For example, a school census may reveal the growth and shifting of school age population, requiring reconsideration of attendance areas assigned to each building and a possible need for new construction. Revenue forecasts will have to be made and faculty committees consulted before approving a new salary schedule. Surveys and polls will be in order before final determination of any significant shift in curricular requirements.

Another important function of the board of education is to serve as the school's spokesman in dealing with other agencies and with the community at large. For example, what policy should govern participation of school musical units in local parades and meetings? When should they be sent on trips to represent the community?

A school code is of great assistance in guiding decisions. This is a document constructed by the board, outlining the curriculum and its goals, school board procedures, administrative structure and responsibilities, contractual obligations of and to the faculty and staff, regulations affecting students, use of buildings and equipment, and community relationships. If wisely constructed and consulted, such an outline answers many questions before they arise, and helps to provide stability to a school's operation.

The governing board of a college or university usually goes under the title of Board of Regents, Board of Governors, Board of Trustees, and the like. It differs from the local school board in its selection, the members normally being appointed by the appropriate state officials or by officers of the supporting religious denomination, municipality, or educational corporation. The governing board therefore maintains close communication with the legislative and executive bodies with which the institution is affiliated. There is also a widespread dialog between the board and the alumni, contributors, or taxpayers who help support the institution. Open meetings are a great help in this regard.

Just as in the case of the local school board, the university governing board is responsible for planning, policy formation, and appraisal of the entire operation. It authorizes and approves, but does not ordinarily concern itself with specific managerial problems.

THE INSTITUTIONAL EXECUTIVE

The most important appointment made by an educational board of control is the executive head of the institution—the school superintendent, university president, or chancellor. Unlike the board members themselves, who devote part time to their school jobs, the executive is a full time employee, entrusted with the operational management of the school program. Yet this individual's authority is seldom spelled out by law. He operates mostly in terms of precedent and the logical assumption of responsibility as permitted by the board. The post is not required but only authorized, and his term of office is determined by the board that appoints him. In most cases, his salary is negotiated separately, rather than being part of the faculty salary schedule.

The role of the school executive officer is to (1) exercise leadership in defining goals, (2) set up the organization to accomplish those ends, (3) recommend measures to procure resources, and (4) allocate resources to produce the best results. This implies close liaison with the board and with the heads of various services within the organization.

Since this field of action is so broad, the school superintendent or university president must have a generalist's approach to the job. Although his professional career was originally based upon specialization in some academic field, experience and attitude have given him a generalists's approach. He may also have acquired certain interests and skills in one or more phases of the job, such as fiscal management or public relations, but he must strive to achieve the balanced, overall point of view. This is necessary if he is to avoid bogging down in detail or directing his energies to the promotion of one phase of the program to the exclusion of others. Above all, the chief executive officer must be a man of vision and a man of action who knows what he stands for and works steadily to accomplish it.

The chief executive works primarily through those he appoints as assistant superintendents or vice presidents and with their subordinates, the principals or deans. He also works closely with another group of personnel who are not assigned directly to instructional units; these are staff positions which serve to advise the chief executive officer and to accomplish certain specialized services. These will include the business office, library, registrar, counseling and testing, information and scheduling, extension, food services, transportation, and the like. In the local school systems, supervisors and consultants in special subject areas are also part of the administrative staff. The authority of these staff officers over the general faculty extends only as far as it is specifically defined by their own executive officer. Strictly speaking, therefore, the music supervisor as a staff officer has no direct responsibility for hiring music personnel, assigning their responsibilities, budgeting and purchasing music supplies, and so on. He may be asked to advise and prepare recommendations on these matters and these recommendations may be adopted —and thus he may find himself occupied with executive responsibilities— but this is in addition to his inherent job of direct assistance to the teachers in their job of music teaching.

Having organized the school personnel and delegated tasks as needed, the chief executive officer mediates and coordinates the work of his administrative team. Thus, he must know when to advise and correct, when to assist and when to reassign tasks, and when to redefine responsibilities or institute new procedures or new programs. There is very little to guide him in his job except his personal conception of the school's potential and his exploration of the manner in which the situation is developing. Any major moves must be cleared in advance with the board.

The "top man" is necessarily placed upon a pedestal. He tends to exemplify the institution and serves as a rallying point for its supporters. The institution is fortunate which has a chief executive with sufficient magnetism to unify and motivate the entire organization.

DEAN OF FINE ARTS

As we have just stated, a key position in the university music program is discharged by the dean who is appointed by the president or academic vice-president to manage the programs in music and related disciplines. The combinations range from the basic performing arts—music, theatre, and dance—to include all the fine arts, communications, and the humanities. Thus, music may be ranged with theatre, art, design, architecture, speech, radio and television, photography, journalism, English, foreign languages, and philosophy. Sometimes, instead, the music department is included in the college of Arts and Sciences, or in the college of Education as one of the teaching specialties. The actual grouping is really a matter of organizational evolution and administrative convenience, calculated to achieve a group of manageable size and balance. Whatever the actual grouping, music becomes one of a set of disciplines budgeted and administered through one office.

The dean's job is middle management. He is not properly involved in the daily operational decisions of his various academic units, for he must take care to avoid interfering in jobs which he has already delegated. At the same time, he is not often required to give a public accounting of needs and achievements in his sector as his superior, the president, must do.

Yet the function of the dean's office is critical to the university music program. Initially, it receives and assigns the resources necessary to support the music program. To do this effectively, it must achieve a realistic understanding of the goals, needs, and capabilities of the music unit, along with a similar understanding of the other academic units within its province.

As an outgrowth of its assignment of resources, the dean's office provides centralized services that are impractical for the individual units. These may include certain secretarial services, detailed accounting, etc. Normally, all official business is routed through the dean's office.

Another primary function of the dean's office is the power of intercession. It serves to protect the music department and the other component units from bureaucratic insensitivity and the competitive forces at work within any large educational institution. In short, the dean "pulls his rank" to overcome roadblocks and bottlenecks which interfere with the legitimate aspirations of the music department; he champions music's interests against outside forces which threaten to hamper the music program.

Perhaps the most important function of the dean is that of judicious review of the departmental operation, and the modification or correction of any unwise decision. In other words, the dean should be relied upon, if he is properly consulted, to save the department from any significant misstep. This is why he assists in interviewing prospective faculty members, and processes all recommendations for promotions, new courses and new curricula, and so on. It is the dean's responsibility to assess the probable consequences of any move, and to react accordingly with his vigorous support or a firm veto. He must also exercise his power to suspend any ongoing project which appears to be headed in the wrong direction. This same review function applies particularly to the position of the department chairman, who must be relieved of the post by the dean when it becomes clear to him that the incumbent lacks the ability or consensus necessary to function effectively.

THE BUILDING PRINCIPAL

The building principal of an elementary or secondary school occupies a position analogous to that of university dean. It is a middle management job, lying between the superintendent and the various teachers. Like a dean, he is called upon to assign available resources, to provide centralized services, to protect the weak and curb the strong, and to oversee the instructional programs with an eye to stimulating promising developments and modifying or correcting those moves which seem to require it.

But the principal's job is identified with the entire educative program carried on within one building, as contrasted with the dean's concern with a group of related departments perhaps widely spread about a campus; hence, it is a task at once more comprehensive and yet more directly involved with instruction in the individual classroom. A large proportion of the principal's effort is therefore supervisory in the sense that he carries on an active effort toward the improvement of instruction; in other words, he observes instruction in progress and works with the teachers, organizes workshops and other in-service educational activity, and generally assists in promoting better teaching plans and techniques. Sharing this supervisory load with him are the various supervisors and consultants in the special subjects, including music. But the work of the supervisory staff is coordinated with and through him since departmentalization is not usually as strong at the elementary and secondary levels as it is in the university.

THE MUSIC EXECUTIVE

Most school systems have one or more individuals designated as music supervisor. This post may be entrusted to one individual, but the task is often decentralized to the extent of naming separate supervisors for the vocal and instrumental music programs or for the elementary and secondary levels. If the title were strictly interpreted, these music supervisors would be concerned only with the improvement of instruction; the job would consist of working closely with the other music specialists and the classroom teachers and their students to upgrade the music program. Such a role employs all possible means to analyze the music program, to discover its strengths and weaknesses, to enlist outside support, to consult and advise teaching personnel, to expedite the better employment of effective methods and materials, and to stimulate teachers and students to stronger effort. Music supervision calls for much activity in the classroom, observing and consulting with the teachers, assisting with daily lesson plans, demonstrating new methods and materials, and attending to the in-service growth of the music instructors.[2]

However, it has already been noted that a good many music supervisors have been given or have assumed executive responsibility for their school's music program. This occurs because of the special nature of the field of music, and because the music supervisor is the natural leader of the program. Lacking expertise in the field, the superintendent and principals rely heavily upon their music supervisor and the music teachers regard him as their spokesman. Since it is so generally believed that music programs do not readily conform to standard procedures, making necessary many modifications and exceptions, it seems easiest for everyone to go directly to the leading authority, the music supervisor.

The competent music supervisor usually welcomes this opportunity to exert a more direct control over the music program. The danger lies in the conflict of interest with the principal's office and with the other academic fields. The supervisor must walk circumspectly, therefore, always going "through channels" and doing nothing which might be interpreted as exceeding the limits of his authority.

The titles Chairman, Head, Coordinator, and Director are often used to denote the executive officer of a school music program in larger systems where numerous specialists and consultants are employed and where centralized authority for the music program is desired. Such titles are also used in institutions of higher education, where highly specialized faculty are employed and the supervisory function thus becomes of secondary importance.

There are some slight or imagined connotations associated with these various titles due largely to historical circumstance. Most academic units within American colleges and universities have been organized as departments with designated heads or chairmen. But the prestigious European and American music conservatories and schools, which were originally independent establishments, have ordinarily been headed by

---

2 For detailed treatment of the task of music supervision, see Charles Leonhard and Robert W. House, *Foundations and Principles of Music Education,* 2nd ed. (New York: McGraw-Hill Book Company, 1972), chap. 10.

a director. As university music departments have grown, therefore, they have aspired to the status of school of music with a director. In such a case, further subdivision usually occurs in the form of departments or divisions of voice, keyboard, orchestral instruments, theory and literature, music education, and the like. Thus, a directorship often implies a more autonomous and sizable operation than a chairmanship. But this is no universal rule and all these titles remain in flexible usage.

In any case, the executive officer of the music unit is clearly charged with the administration of the music program within his institution and his purpose is to provide the facilities for instruction. He is clearly a line officer, unlike the school music supervisor, and is delegated the necessary authority to discharge his responsibilities. He seeks out the natural objectives of his program, ascertains its needs, establishes policies and plans, presents recommendations to his superiors to secure the required resources, and directs and controls the operational effort. His task covers the acquisition of qualified faculty members and their assignment, promotion, etc. He must see that the necessary courses are offered and scheduled, that policies governing students are instituted and enforced, that funds are allocated and properly expended, and that all musical activities are well coordinated. In short, he must provide the ultimate direction and decision for the music unit.

Of course, the relative size and historical development of the music unit will somewhat affect the specific duties of the music executive officer. When he has a significant teaching load or where the size of the music faculty exceeds the normal span of control, an executive assistant is usually appointed to assume part of the administrative task. In quite large institutions, where subdivision of the music unit occurs, many executive functions are delegated to the heads of these sub-divisions; in such case, the music chairman actually assumes many of the functions of a dean. Conversely, in small institutions, there is a tendency for the fine arts dean or school principal to retain a more active role in decision-making for the music unit. But, since the music program is essentially unique and indivisible, it is generally the case that the chief executive officer for music is expected to discharge the essential responsibilities for management of that unit.

Music Teachers

All music instructors at various times find themselves involved in administrative duties as they deal with curricular problems, student complaints and requests, space and equipment needs, and so on. This fact is especially true of the directors of musical performing organizations due to the numbers of students involved and the public performances which must be planned, rehearsed, and executed. In effect, much of the administrative task has to be delegated to the operational level because the director is intimately acquainted with the organizational detail surrounding his job.

Typically, therefore, a band director is expected to take his own measures to recruit players, select dates for public appearances, select and order his music, determine his needs for additional instruments and other equipment, check out and check in the instruments, keep an inventory, and arrange for repairs. As a performance or tour approaches, he initiates publicity, sends program copy to the printer, manages ticket sales, plans the itinerary, secures transportation, and supervises the movement of personnel and equipment to the performance site. This is all in addition to the business of direct instruction through the regular rehearsal of his players. Similar responsibilities pertain to the directors of orchestras, choral groups, music theatre and opera.

It is seldom the case that directors of musical performing groups require much prompting in the exercise of their administrative tasks. Indeed, they are likely to overextend their delegated authority to make decisions under pressure of public performance and the maintenance of quality and morale of their organizations. This is apt to produce last-minute extra rehearsals, unheralded cancellation of scheduled appearances, and even unauthorized equipment purchases. In this case, the limits of delegated authority have not been understood or enforced.

In addition to the organization directors, numerous other teachers are engaged in music instruction. These include the university teachers of theoretical and historical courses, courses in music education, vocal and instrumental lessons, and introductory courses in music for the general student. The category also includes instructors of general music in the elementary and secondary schools as well as those who teach music in their own self-contained elementary classrooms. Unless they are assigned a coordinative function, these people may be administratively involved only to the extent of securing the needed resources for their own classes. Along with the organization directors, however, they are the producers of the musical behaviors which form the objectives of the music program. To get the job done, it is imperative that the music teachers work closely with the supervisory and administrative personnel of the school.

ADMINISTRATIVE LEADERSHIP

Implicit in our discussion has been the fact that he who must plan, organize, and control groups is necessarily a leader and must be chosen on that basis. It has also been suggested that leadership is not an exclusive property of those who are so selected, for the qualities of leadership may come to the surface in anyone who sees a problem and who can define its solution and work with others to that end. Within an organization, therefore, informal and unofficial groupings will occur under the leadership of individuals of proven ingenuity. Although this force is useful in many instances, the fact can also be dangerous to the organization to the extent that this energy is not constructively used and channeled into effort which contributes to the goals of the organization.

Since leadership must be supplied, it behooves the organization to identify those, both from within and from without, who most clearly possess it and who may be expected to exercise it most usefully at some point within the administrative structure. Because of the critical nature of this search, numerous attempts have been made to define leadership traits and to establish methods for ascertaining whether these are present in an individual. The most usual method has been by the process of "natural selection." In the case of educational institutions, this has meant that young and vigorous teachers have been placed on committees, given assignments to handle special projects, observed carefully, and then moved into low level administrative posts as vacancies occur and their superiors have moved upward. Seniority within the institution has a natural influence upon this process since there is more time for the benefits of experience to accrue and for reliable observation to take place. Sheer professional competence is obviously a prime consideration in generating authentic goals and in meriting the respect of one's colleagues. Professional activity and the possession of higher academic degrees have also been factors since these are somewhat related to one's professional commitment and prestige. Another factor in choosing educational administrators seems to lie in their particular field of specialization; it will be noted, for example, that athletic coaches are often tapped for such positions because they are experienced in handling equipment and financial problems and in leading groups of people. They are also well acquainted with the problem of public relations and have wide acquaintance within the local community and surrounding area. Their names are well known. For some of these same reasons, directors of musical organizations are the most likely to be selected for administrative posts within the music program.

One of the principal difficulties with this method of securing administrators is, of course, that it leads to the charge of favoritism, or politics, for it may appear to the other faculty members that the selected individual has been "bucking" for the promotion. It is also possible that the qualities which made the individual a likely candidate—experience, degrees, and devotion to his discipline—have molded him in such a way that he does not see the problems fairly and objectively in a wider context. In short, he has become too specialized and his goals are too narrow.

In the attempt to avoid these dangers, some institutions have begun by listing leadership traits, which list can include any ten or twenty adjectives descriptive of traits thought to be desirable. The list of available personnel is then combed by means of questionnaires in order to determine those who possess the best profiles for leadership. Tests may be given, and leadership schools employed as in the armed services and in some industrial organizations.

Although experience in assessing leadership traits has not proved exceptionally reliable, certain characteristics do seem to show a positive correlation with successful leadership. These are:

1. Above-average intelligence
2. Broad, well-rounded interests
3. Unusual verbal facility, written and/or spoken
4. Mental and emotional maturity
5. Powerful inner drive
6. Cooperative ability

However, it is still true that the generalized qualities of leadership do not necessarily fit one for a specific administrative post. Although top management in large corporations is often shifted so that the production manager successfully moves to sales management, and the U.S. Undersecretary of State may become Secretary of Defense in another administration, the usual administrative position in an educational institution demands quite intimate acquaintance with the problems and procedures to be faced. Even more true is the fact that one school or one music department may require a different brand of leadership than another does, due to differing personnel, problems, and goals.

Since neither natural selection nor the traitist approach is infallible, many educational institutions have found success in combining both principles—spotting those who seem to show leadership ability, giving them responsible tasks to test their abilities, and then matching their traits to the requirements of any new administrative openings. Many mistakes are also avoided by the method of "internship," whereby the most promising candidate is placed as an assistant or associate of the retiring administrator, taking over gradually during a period of one or two years.

The optimum time to occupy a particular administrative post seems to vary widely. Of course, the unsuccessful individual should be relieved of the job as soon as his incapacity proves obvious. But highly successful administrators can also outlive their usefulness, having solved the kinds of problems they can meet, and failing to make progress on others. Estimates of the period of optimum productiveness in a post range from five to fifteen years, and must depend upon the specific circumstances.

At some such point, however, most successful administrators would be best promoted or transferred to another post within the institution or in a different locality.

The exercise of leadership ultimately depends upon satisfaction of the needs of followers. That is to say that the activities of the unit must accomplish objectives that are within the power of the group, thus achieving that which the group considers desirable and which results in some increase in the personal satisfaction of the individual members of the group. In order to accomplish this, an administrator needs to understand that individuals have personal objectives which are not identical with those of the organization. A brief list of these includes security, clear-cut responsibilities, good working conditions, adequate supervision, satisfactory personal relationships, a sense of accomplishment, recognition and status, opportunity for growth and advancement. It is necessary for the administrator to concern himself with these items, and to demonstrate how they relate to the achievement of the objectives of the institution. It is a cyclic relationship; theoretically, a "happy shop" will produce a good team effort toward better educational outcomes, which in turn will secure higher salaries, improved teaching facilities, recognition and advancement. In practice, however, school salaries are increasingly tied to a schedule and other external rewards are insufficient to go around. What remains within the power of the administrator to provide are perhaps a better desk, a prized committee assignment, expenses to a convention, and the "green light" to proceed with a pet project. Even so, such items can demonstrate the administrator's confidence in the individual and that conditions can improve if a good job is done. Conversely, those whose work is inferior or destructive in terms of organizational objectives need to be warned, disciplined, and finally removed.

More fundamentally, the administrator needs to extend participation in successful group endeavor and to delegate authority and responsibility to the lowest level consistent with effective operations. Fortunately, in this case, he is dealing with professional people, whose dedication to professional ideals is sometimes amazing. Music department faculty members, for example, often exhibit a built-in drive to establish a growing, flourishing department second to none. They will labor long hours over many years to find talented students, and to teach them and counsel them toward a brilliant career in music. They will spend untold hours building a fine performing group and in planning and preparing its appearances. Such dedication is the rule and not the exception. And the administrator who can help them accomplish these things is sure to be followed.

The by-product of successful administrative leadership is good unit morale and a free hand in planning, organizing, and controlling the operation. The members of such an organization will believe in its central mission and will know that the group effort will be self-rewarding. They will be comfortable in their own jobs and will be proud to identify with the group. They will work harmoniously and will have confidence in the organization and in its leadership. Most importantly, they will be producing superior educational outcomes; this is the goal which the properly functioning administrator seeks for his school's music program.

QUESTIONS FOR DISCUSSION

1. How does the function of administration relate to instruction and to supervision?

2. Describe the managerial process and its relation to educational administration. What is the inherent distinction between the administrative and the operational levels?

3. What is the nature of managerial planning? What are its natural elements? Who assists the administrator in this task?

4. Define and illustrate the relationships among line and staff organization. How far does the authority of staff officers extend?

5. Describe how educational systems develop organizational patterns through growth and division of responsibility. What are some of the reasons for organizational decentralization?

6. Define responsibility, authority, and accountability. How may one remain accountable without holding direct responsibility?

7. Distinguish between administrative control and operative control. Review the steps involved in the control process.

8. What is the extent of administrative involvement of federal and state agencies with the schools and colleges? What role is fulfilled by local governing boards?

9. Characterize the job of the school superintendent or college president. How does his role relate to those of his deans or principals and to the music program?

10. What are the inherent tasks of the music executive officer? How are these affected by the size of his unit? What administrative responsibilities are commonly delegated to music teachers?

11. How are good administrators identified? How does the exercise of leadership relate to the needs of the faculty? What approaches will help to produce united effort?

SUGGESTED READINGS

Davis, Ralph C. *The Fundamentals of Top Management.* New York: Harper & Row, Publishers, 1951.

Flippo, Edwin B., *Management: A Behavioral Approach,* 2nd ed. Boston: Allyn and Bacon, 1970.

Koontz, Harold, and Cyril O'Donnell, *Principles of Management,* 2nd ed. New York: McGraw-Hill Book Company, Inc., 1959.

Leonhard, Charles, and Robert W. House, *Foundations and Principles of Music Education,* 2nd ed. New York: McGraw-Hill Book Company, Inc., 1972, chaps. 9–10.

Morphet, Edgar L., Roe L. Johns, and Theodore L. Reller, *Educational Organization and Administration,* 2nd ed. Englewood Cliffs, N.J.: Prentice-Hall, Inc. 1967, chaps. 8–13.

Newman, William H., *Administrative Action,* 2nd ed. Englewood Cliffs, N.J.: Prentice-Hall, Inc., 1963.

Sears, Jesse B., *The Nature of the Administrative Process.* New York: McGraw-Hill Book Company, Inc. 1950.

CHAPTER THREE

building the music curriculum

The school curriculum is defined as all the activities sponsored by the school and the resultant learning experiences which are achieved by the individual student. To put it another way, it consists of whatever a student does and perceives during the entire period of his schooling, which he would not have done or perceived had he not been enrolled and attending the school. This broad definition includes the influences which stem from a student's attendance in class, his homework and musical practice, all extracurricular and social activities, and the formal and informal contacts with the teachers and school officials and with his fellow students. The final results of these influences constitute the outcomes of schooling.

Thus it is that a student who is not actually enrolled in a music course, nor participating directly in any musical activity within his classes, is nevertheless affected by the musical activities of the school as he attends school programs and athletic events where music is provided, and whenever musical topics are discussed by his teachers and classmates. We, of course, are especially concerned with the musical portion of the curriculum and its component parts—the band program, the string program, the choral program, the general music program at all levels, and all the undergraduate and graduate degree programs in music which may be encountered in institutions of higher learning. Because musical activity is so pervasive, it must be carefully established and adjusted within the total curriculum of a school.

It is not profitable in a book of this kind to review in detail the "standard" music curriculum, since this information is contained in many books relating to music education. What is important is to outline the way in which administrative measures are taken in order to create the kind of curriculum which any particular educational institution may desire and deserve to have. What are the administrative responsibilities in this regard, and how may they be accomplished?

It should be clear that curriculum building is much more than determining offerings and credit allotment, and establishing requirements, although these are all part of the process. *The actual content of a subject and the ways in which students are led to approach it, is the key factor.* Remembering that the curriculum is the instrument by which the institution will produce its outcomes, the administrative role is to see that the musical needs of the students are determined, cast in the form of objectives, and the appropriate activities planned, organized, and controlled to these ends. It is not enough to say that "most schools have bands, so we will have one," and to secure the band director and the necessary facilities to produce one. Indeed, most schools *do* possess bands, but the results of these programs vary widely; in some cases a great deal of musicianship is produced and in other cases very little of lasting value is ever accomplished. The reason for this is that different styles and approaches are employed in operating these various band programs, all under the guidance of differing administrative philosophy and technique.

DEVELOPING OBJECTIVES

The development of objectives is the first step in curriculum building. They serve to assure consistency with broad educational aims, in planning educative experiences, in ordering instruction, and in establishing a basis for evaluation. The first chapter dealt broadly with the topic, claiming music as one of the basic elements of living and therefore as one of the essential components of schooling. Certain forms of musicianship were suggested as appropriate targets for general education. These become objectives common to most music programs, simply because they flow from the constancy of human nature and the inherent approaches to the art of music—listening, performing, analyzing, and creating.

But the objectives of each school must and will differ from other schools due to its unique combination of students and resources; each institution must take into account the level and quality of its own student body, the type and capability of the faculty, and the time and money available for the task. Thus, the objectives of an inner city school will differ materially from those of a suburban school only a few miles away, and still different outcomes will be sought in a small rural school. Differing clientele will also be found in a small liberal arts college and a large music conservatory. Each institution must strive to serve its own student body in its own way. Thus, the formulation of objectives is a formidable task, involving thorough understanding of the process and much teamwork in completing the task.

LEVELS OF OBJECTIVES

What is an objective? Much confusion is swept away when it is understood that objectives are of different level and application, and that they are formulated by different individuals and groups. The *broad social objectives* of education have been established by society and are subject to gradual modification. They are the product of infinite evaluation of man's needs and social condition. The result is a working consensus that the business of the schools is to provide certain values inherent to the needs of that society, such as self-sufficiency through knowledge and economic efficiency, individual freedom, and democratic institutions. Such goals are formulated by political and educational philosophers, as the result of much searching analysis of societal directions. Recent moves within our educational institutions for racial integration and equality of educational opportunity constitute a response to modifications in our concept of the broad social objectives.

The *concrete social objectives* of education constitute the attempt by the schools to define major qualities of citizens which must be produced if society's charge to the schools is to be met. Objectives of this level are to be found on such lists as the "Seven Cardinal Principles of Education," and the "Purposes of Education in American Democracy," both quoted in our first chapter. The formulation of such statements is usually accomplished by educational authorities representing the establishment. One effect of these is to provide a model for the individual statement of objectives adopted by each educational institution. Another effect is the implied definition of the subjects to be included within the curriculum. Thus, the objective of Health implies that there shall be a program in health and physical education; the objective of Esthetic Interests implies that there shall be programs in music, art, drama, and literature.

Program objectives are those which give direction to each subject matter area. They define the attributes of a successful graduate of the institution, stated in behavioral terms. The objectives of the National Assessment Program in music, listed in our first chapter, outlines such behaviors on a national basis, indicating the kinds of musical knowledge, understanding, skills, attitudes, and appreciations believed to be appropriate to any high school graduate. These include the ability to read and perform music, skill in listening, knowledge of standard musical literature and its historical background, a concept of its structural features, a sense of musical taste, and a liking for musical participation. Each item on this list, or any other, has to be examined for its application to the particular institution. This is the collective responsibility of the music faculty and its administrators.

Instructional objectives are the carefully defined goals of each course or activity. The beginning string class, for example, will most likely be concerned with achieving elemental skills in tuning and caring for the instrument, facility with basic bowing and fingering patterns, command of notation, accurate rhythm and intonation, good practice habits, and a desire to continue instruction. Achievement of these leads to membership in the school orchestra where these behaviors are to be reinforced, extended, and refined, but where one expects also to achieve good ensemble habits, fine tone, expressive playing, and wide acquaintance with good orchestral literature. Of course, at the same time, the general elementary music program and other musical exposure undergone by these orchestra players should finally combine to produce the broad, well-rounded musical behaviors sought for all the school's graduates. In other words, the instructional objectives are limited, short-term goals, largely contrived by the individual instructor to meet the immediate needs of his students but which also contribute to the objectives of the entire music program.

The needs of students, in turn, are primarily cast in terms of *personal objectives*. These derive from their need for security, status, satisfactory personal relationships, group membership, and self-fulfillment. Fortunately, music is a subject where fulfillment of these needs is usually available. A particular student's objective may be to win the solo contest or to make first chair in his section. He may also develop vocational ambitions in music, or he may merely be seeking more satisfactory personal and group relationships than are possible in his other subjects. Such goals are seldom stated and often not consciously held. If the curriculum is to be fully effective, however, conditions must be such that these student objectives are perceived by the faculty and opportunity provided the student to achieve those which are complementary to those of the school.

Formulating Objectives

In spite of much talk about them, most objectives are assumed. The individual teacher thinks he knows very well what his subject is all about, and proceeds to go after it. The trouble is that others do not always hold the same assumptions. This is why music personnel in a school are often observed to be working at a furious pace but at cross-purposes with one another, and hardly sensing the nature of the problem. One individual may naturally assume that the idea is to make the organization sound just as well as possible, while his colleague believes that music should be fun. Another may have the notion that the job is to create *esprit de corps* and involve everyone in music, while yet another may just as firmly believe in talent selection and sheer work. There is certainly room for such differences of opinion but they must be reconciled; this is where administration comes in.

It is a commonly accepted idea that administration provides the resources but that the faculty determines the curriculum. This is only partially true, in the sense that the teacher does the work of instruction and thus activates the curriculum. But a properly coordinated curriculum, rather than a "free school," requires joint planning by faculty members and their administrators, seeking to establish overall philosophy and effective objectives, followed by instruction organized on those terms.

Objectives, therefore, cannot well be assumed; they must be properly formulated. Whenever this occurs, however, there is danger that they will be idealistic and impractical, reflecting only what the writer thinks they *ought* to be. Then, since it is difficult to quibble with one's colleague, the group may tend to accept the statement "in principle" and simply continue to operate on their personal assumptions.

There is no remedy for this except through adept administrative direction. What the administrator needs to do is to establish channels for some very substantive dialog among members of his unit. Working in committees or as a committee of the whole, the music faculty must be led to reexamine the professional literature pertaining to the objectives of music instruction and to reevaluate their program's possible contribution to the objectives of their institution. Provision for student input should be made. Gradually, if the process is carefully nurtured, some central beliefs will emerge as a true consensus. These central beliefs, in their turn, become the basis for identifying valid program objectives, which must be written down provisionally for review and study.

If, for example, it appears to be agreed that the local student body has a general acquaintance with current popular forms, but that little attention is being paid by them to their significant musical heritage, then the need for objectives to remedy this defect becomes apparent. Broad acquaintance with standard musical literature through the general music classes and performing organizations becomes a logical objective— and so does a working knowledge of music's structure and historical evolution. These objectives may immediately suggest the need for more extensive and intensive music listening activity in the early grades. They may also suggest the need for an extension of the general music require- ment and a recasting of its content to make the necessary bridge between the students' understanding of current popular styles and the earlier jazz forms, followed by a study of primitive and classical dance forms and their development into symphonic forms. Similar revisions in the litera- ture to be studied and performed by the large organizations may be indicated. The formation of additional stage bands and other small en- sembles may also be thought appropriate. A series of school assembly programs by these various performing groups may be planned to rein- force and extend this effort.

Working onward from here, the administrator should seek to draw attention to other gaps in the music program. Are the students being given sufficient encouragement to learn to play an instrument and sing in groups? If not, what does this suggest about the need for a regular program of keyboard instruction in the early grades, followed by instruc- tion on song flute or recorder, the institution of a string program, addi- tional beginning band instrument classes, and the formation of additional choral groups open to all students?

Gradually, a comprehensive body of objectives should emerge covering the essential items of musical knowledge, understanding, atti- tudes, appreciations, and skills which need to be promoted in each major area of the program. This process of identifying and formulating objec- tives is treated in detail by Charles Leonhard and Robert House in *Foundations and Principles of Music Education*.[1] Of course, the ad- ministrator must be aware that the newly developing music curriculum may require additional staff and resources and organizational readjust- ment in the form of class scheduling and space allotment. His participa- tion in the process of curriculum development assumes the fact that he will be working to provide the necessary means to achieve the goals that he has helped to set. The individual faculty member, for his part, be- comes responsible to translate the program objectives into instructional objectives—those specific items of musical behavior which he will pro- mote in his own classes—and to develop the necessary instructional content and methods to produce them in his students. The administra-

---

[1] New York: McGraw-Hill Book Company, 2nd ed., 1972, chap. 6.

tion, largely through adequate supervision, attempts to aid each teacher to discharge this obligation.

It can be seen that this entire process of developing objectives must be continuous, and under periodic administrative stimulation, in order to meet the needs of a changing student body and faculty and the continued evolution of music literature and its methodology.

While working to give direction to his unit's effort to achieve a meaningful body of objectives, the administrator must seek to establish the operational basis for the faculty and students to do the job. Aside from providing the needed faculty members and student personnel services, the required space and equipment, and fiscal machinery—which topics will be treated in later chapters—he must see that the other curricular arrangements are achieved. These include the development of specific courses and activities to be offered or required, the arrangement of these into a practical daily schedule where instruction can proceed with proper space and equipment, and the provision of necessary adjuncts to instruction. In dealing with these items, the administrator must proceed on the principle that the teacher needs to be relieved as much as possible of peripheral activity, in order to devote his entire energy to the creative job of instruction.

ESTABLISHING OFFERINGS
AND REQUIREMENTS

The Elementary Curriculum in Music

It has already been stated that the naming of courses and credits is of little value here, because these are already outlined by accrediting bodies and treated extensively in the professional literature. This is especially true at the elementary school level, since music is traditionally handled as an undifferentiated core subject and included within each day's activities. The typical course of study includes singing, playing, listening, rhythmic, and creative activities. The content is arranged sequentially from week to week and from grade to grade, in accordance with the developing maturity and musical awareness of the pupils. Superimposed upon this basic course are special elective offerings in instrumental instruction leading to participation in the school's instrumental ensembles.

Again, this elementary music program cannot be trusted to work itself out properly without administrative guidance. Having seen to the development of adequate objectives, the administration must first ask "who will do the job?" Will instruction in this school be most effectively handled by the music specialists, by the classroom teachers, or by some working combination of the two? The usual arguments on both sides of this question are of little help to the administrator on the spot. Having some idea of the job to be accomplished and of the qualifications of his available teaching staff, he must decide who shall be assigned the job. When he has sufficient strength in terms of special music teachers, he can rely upon them—and if not, he must ascertain which classroom teachers are most capable of it and assign them the task. In many cases, this will mean that some classroom teachers in the primary grades will be teaching music for more than one classroom, while their colleagues are handling other subjects for them. This plan, in effect, modifies the principle of the self-contained classroom in favor of partial departmentalization.

In ungraded schools further departmentalization occurs. What happens is that pupils are recruited from all age levels for various musical projects and activities such as music reading, beginning instrumental classes and individual lessons, small vocal and instrumental ensembles, rhythm and dance groups, individual and group listening sessions, and the like. In this kind of climate, special activities for the handicapped, the slow learner, and the gifted student are more readily arranged. All of these activities are coordinated and supervised by qualified specialists.

A further element in good curricular planning involves the integration or correlation of music with other subjects at appropriate points. Thus, in planning units in social studies and literature and in developing projects such as plays and skits, teachers should be encouraged to consider the inclusion of appropriate musical activity.

Throughout the program of general music in the elementary grades the administrative concern is to see that a balanced, thorough approach is maintained. The teachers must not be allowed to get by with a minimal program consisting of the sporadic presentation and review of rote-learned songs. A complete diet of good music literature must be studied. There should also be a deliberately organized program of instruction in the classroom instruments, keyboard experiences, song flutes and fretted instruments, and sequential music reading activity. Music listening sessions should be carefully planned to maximize the understanding of music's structure and historical development. Above all, flexible presentation must allow for the kind of pupil improvisation and creativity which has long been sponsored by our cousins who teach Art in the elementary schools.

Coming to the field of specialized instrumental instruction, the administrator must make certain that all pupils who wish to study a band or orchestral instrument, or piano, have opportunity to do so. This means effective administrative measures to ensure that the offer is properly made and left open at each ensuing grade level. It means that instruments will be supplied as required and that pupils' schedules will be arranged to allow a convenient organization of these groups. At the same time, special care is needed to make certain that the instrumental instructors are accomplishing more than rudimentary performance technique. Unthinking drill has no place in instruction. These classes must also be directed toward the achievement of expressive playing, acquaintance with worthwhile literature, and, through successful endeavor, to the desire to continue participation in musical activities.

THE SECONDARY CURRICULUM IN MUSIC

The junior and senior high school curriculum in music is usually characterized by the tapering off of general music as a universal requirement, coupled with the expansion of elective offerings in the form of advanced performing groups and specialized courses in music theory, history, etc. In many localities, general music or music appreciation is required in the seventh grade or in the seventh and eighth grades as the students' last formal contact with music. This being the case, a massive effort is needed to make this course come alive. Unfortunately, the opposite is usually the case; those who elect a performing organization are usually excused and the remainder, who have mostly remained indifferent to serious music, are organized into large classes and put through the rudiments of music once again under the leadership of teachers who complain that they would rather be teaching band, orchestra, or chorus.

This poisonous situation must not be allowed to continue. Either the class must be dropped and perhaps reinstituted as an elective for high school seniors, or it must be organized to ensure that it provides a fitting capstone to the program in general music. If the latter is to be the case, it will need to be required of all students including the members of performing groups, and scheduled in such a way that they may still participate in the elective performing group; this probably means scheduling general music twice a week for two years, with the organizations meeting on the alternate days. Secondly, the most vigorous, creative teachers must be assigned to the course. Finally, the course needs to be centered upon the active study of the major forms and eras of musical composition. It should not be a watered-down music history course; it should be devoted to the examination in depth of a few representative musical compositions. The students should become familiar with the major signposts of musical style and design, so they may finally achieve the ability to listen to unfamiliar compositions with insight and interest.

This same ability is an inherent goal of the secondary school performing groups. It should be made easier of accomplishment by reason of the necessity for each student to involve himself directly in the musical detail as a performer. But the opposite is often the case as the director finds himself pressed to prepare only for the public performance. The dilemma is that while performance can be the most effective agent of musical learning, the effort is easily diverted to the ends of professionalism and entertainment. It has to be remembered that, in contrast with professional performing groups, the entertainment of audiences is not a true objective but a side effect of instruction. The actual pursuit of musicianship is carried on in rehearsals, and the approaching public presentation functions as an incentive to make the process more meaningful. This fact must not be obscured in the natural drive for excellence of performance on the part of directors and their students.

Not only are the directors and participants in the bands, orchestras, and choral groups easily misled in terms of the true objectives of their program, but the public and the school administrators themselves are subject to the same error. They tend to measure results in terms of contest ratings and showmanship on the stage and on the gridiron. And it is difficult to ignore these pressures. The fact is that good public relations *is* an important and desirable concomitant of a flourishing music program. Whenever a public performance is to be given, it *should* be a winner. But how can this be done without distorting the values of the students?

The answer to this problem lies in the attitudes of the directors of the organizations. The true educator will not set impossible standards of perfection or drill his students until they drop. He will keep his eyes glued beyond the performance to the achievement of musicianship by his students; he will be working for their easy facility, expressive playing, sight reading ability, wide acquaintance with the literature, and powers of musical discrimination. In doing this, he will achieve good public performances. But he will not be inordinately proud of these; he will simply note this result as partial evidence of his students' state of development.

The administrator's job is to see that this state of mind is encouraged. He establishes the band, orchestra, and chorus in the curriculum, arranges for their instruction, evaluates the results, and then rewards the achievement of solid musical and educational values. He points to the fine literature these groups are studying and their large repertoires; he compliments their facility and smooth style, observes their sincerity and enthusiasm for music, and notes the numbers of students that continue to participate in music after graduation.

The administrator should also be cognizant of the fact that the large organizations cannot provide the complete range of performing experience. Solo and small ensemble opportunities are a necessity if the music curriculum is to flourish. They allow for the development of leadership and greater facility, style, and interpretative independence. Such activity tends to have strong carryover into musical participation in adult life. Stress in this field in European schools is, incidentally, one of the primary explanations of the relatively high musicality exhibited by European populations.

Luckily, very little is required in order to produce flourishing activity in small ensemble work. Most of the rehearsal is achieved during the students' study hall times, before and after school and at home, and without direct supervision by an instructor. It is largely a matter of organization—securing volunteers, forming compatible groups, supplying appropriate literature, arranging individual schedules to allow group rehearsals, and occasional coaching. Any adequate secondary school music program should include various instrumental and vocal trios, quartets, sextets, stage bands, madrigal groups, percussion ensembles, and separate choirs of string, brass, and woodwind players. All of these should be rehearsing regularly throughout the year. Greater effort from the director is required for the larger groups, because more problems in organization occur and more coaching is needed.

Solo preparation by students can also be managed with a minimum of effort, especially if it is not conceived as the offering of a regular series of private lessons. Full-fledged private instruction is really professional training and is more appropriate to the individual commercial teacher and to the university and conservatory programs for music majors; here, the inherent goals are complete technical mastery and development of the student's solo repertoire. Where this attempt is made in the public schools much wasted motion occurs with those students who do not have professional goals. The school is lucky which has qualified private teachers locally available to whom interested students can be referred; where this is not the case, the school director needs to identify those who can profit from the study of solo literature, find them appropriate solos, coach them occasionally on their interpretation, and provide occasions upon which they can perform.

Another phase of the performing program consists of the occasional preparation and presentation of musicals, operas, and large choral-instrumental works. The administrator should be alert to the possibility, since the desirability of students studying these forms of musical literature is obvious. Problems in management and internal cooperation must be anticipated, but the chief danger lies in an overexpenditure of time and effort. Administrative control needs to be properly exerted to ensure that practical works are selected, that too large a portion of the school year is not occupied in the preparation, and that rehearsal time is not excessive.

Many schools are now offering a humanities course as a junior-senior course supplementing or substituting for the junior high course in general music. Its function is to give an integrated treatment of music and the other arts within a historical setting. Musically, its goals and format should be similar to those of the general music course, with added emphasis upon parallel historical and artistic developments. The administrative problem lies in finding the teacher qualified to handle such a broad field, or in properly coordinating the work of a team of teachers.

In large high schools, where there is sufficient demand from students considering a career in music, it is feasible to offer introductory courses in music history, music theory and composition, conducting, and instrument repair. Where enrollment does not permit the organization of classes, the work can be handled on an individual project basis. The content should be similar to college level courses of the same type, being obviously aimed at the precocious, gifted music student.

THE MUSIC CURRICULUM IN HIGHER EDUCATION

The individual student's program in college is definitely divided into two categories: (1) those subjects which are designed to further liberalize and broaden his background, and (2) those subjects which pertain to his chosen career. Each discipline attempts to serve both needs through required or elective courses in "general education" and programs for career specialization. Since a final career choice is so often delayed, it has been found expedient to concentrate general education in the early years and to increasingly specialize as one progresses through the undergraduate and graduate programs.

The music program for the non-major student is thus comparable to the secondary school program. There is usually a general music course called "Music Understanding" or "Introduction to Music." This course is naturally similar in format to a good junior high school general music course but surely needs to be approached at an appropriately higher intellectual level. The course would not be needed if an adequate job were being done in the elementary and secondary schools. Where it is required, therefore, provision for waiver by proficiency examination is advisable. The usual problem with this course is that class size becomes unwieldy and instruction easily becomes shallow and pedantic.

Other courses for the general student usually treat certain broad types of music, as "Folk Music in America," "The Evolution of Jazz," "Afro-American Music," and "Contemporary Musical Styles." These should function to give the student insight into the style and design of the kinds of music he must deal with as a layman. In addition, certain instrumental and choral organizations are ordinarily open to all volunteers who participated in such groups in high school and who wish to continue even though they are not majoring in music.

It must not be overlooked that a significant force in general education may be provided by the concerts, clinics, lectures, and broadcasts sponsored by the music unit. Insofar as possible, these should be free and open to the entire student body. In many cases, the introductory courses may be coordinated with certain of these events by means of preparatory listening and discussion, joint class attendance, and follow-up reports and critique.

These offerings in general music and the basic performing groups form the core of the program in community colleges or junior colleges. These institutions are designed to provide terminal, two-year programs, as well as preprofessional work for those who will transfer to senior colleges. Generally, music faculties are small and the number of students specializing in music is limited. Beyond the core offerings just mentioned, therefore, instruction is usually limited to one or two years of music theory, a survey course in music literature, beginning class piano, and private lessons in those fields in which the faculty is qualified. Arrangements are often made for part-time instructors in the various applied fields until growing enrollments have resulted in a sufficiently large and specialized full-time staff.

Beyond the music offerings just outlined, senior colleges generally offer certain special courses for the musical preparation of elementary classroom teachers. These include class piano, fundamentals of music, and methods of teaching music in the primary and upper elementary grades. Many institutions also offer further study for these people, in the form of a music minor or a "concentration in music."

The four-year degree programs are of several types, all outlined in the National Association of Schools of Music *By-Laws and Regulations*.[2] For the Bachelor of Music Education program leading to certification for teaching, the student takes approximately one-third of his work in general education, one-half in music, and the remaining one-sixth in professional education including music methods and practice teaching in music. Specialized programs in each of the various instruments and in voice, in music theory and composition, in music history

---

[2] Washington, D.C., the Association, 1965.

and literature, in church music, and in music therapy all reserve about two-thirds of the curriculum for musical study. The major in music for the Bachelor of Arts degree typically prescribes only one-third of the work in music and the remainder is used for requirements and electives in other academic areas; this program is not popular, since it does not give sufficient preparation for most vocations in music.

It will be noted that the musical portion of these programs is extensive in most cases. Historically, music major requirements have been the heaviest among all the disciplines, allowing the least electives and flexibility. This is explained by the fact that most entering students possess little or no theoretical or historical background in music and even their performance skills are only partially developed. The heavy major also stems from the fact that music conservatories had developed intensive programs of instruction, and these patterns were imitated in developing the early curriculum patterns in American universities which were later codified by the National Association of Schools of Music. This situation is not always understood or accepted by other academic personnel wishing to extend academic requirements, and thus the music units are constantly being forced to defend their traditional share of the students' curricula.

The actual degree programs to be offered by an institution will depend upon its size and resources and its particular type of clientele. That is, liberal arts colleges will tend to need music degree programs in performance, history-literature, and liberal arts (B.A. major); small teachers colleges will naturally concentrate upon the degree program in music education; and the large universities and music conservatories will provide a more or less complete choice of programs. The most universal offering, of course, is the degree program in music education, since by far the largest demand is for school music teachers. The next most popular degree programs are in voice, piano, organ, and the various orchestral instruments. In any institution, any further proliferation of degree programs needs to be weighed carefully in terms of student demand and available resources.

Professional programs in music all include two basic components. These are (1) Basic Music including the theoretical and historical phases of music, and (2) Musical Performance including the large and small performing ensembles and private and class instruction in voice and the various instruments. For music education students, a third category consists in the conducting and music methods courses which are coordinated with the work in educational philosophy and psychology and with practice teaching in order to prepare them for music teaching. The outlines of the various degree programs are adjusted to provide for more or less concentration of study within each of these categories.

Any appraisal of the music curriculum usually begins with music theory, since it is considered basic to the student's further development. Here is where he acquires a working familiarity with the language and grammar of music, through aural and visual analysis of representative literature, and by the creative application of rules of practice in notation and at the keyboard. Some institutions have divided this study into separate courses and others have elected to manage it by means of a combined, integrated course covering two or three years. Advanced study in this field usually takes the form of separate courses in analysis and form, counterpoint, arranging, and composition.

A parallel effort is undertaken to inculcate an extensive acquaintance with music literature and its historical evolution. This is usually developed by means of introductory courses in music literature, followed by a chronological survey at the sophomore or junior level, and advanced courses devoted to particular forms or historical periods. Some institutions attempt to combine the historical with the theoretical aspects of music into a large course called "Comprehensive Musicianship."

Much controversy exists regarding the content and sequence of these theoretical and historical subjects. The traditional view is that the program in theory should emphasize fundamental skills in ear training and part writing, beginning with the "common practice" of the eighteenth and early nineteenth centuries, and proceeding as far as possible in the direction of both earlier and later idioms. The history course, on the other hand, has been basically chronological. There is a trend, however, stemming largely from the Contemporary Music Project, to treat these subjects more creatively, drawing out structural principles common to all eras but emphasizing contemporary techniques.

Considerable latitude is thus afforded the music administrator in establishing the program in music theory and history. He will need to consult the actual status of the entering students, the objectives of his unit, and the capabilities and beliefs of his faculty, in order to develop the most practical approach to this phase of the curriculum. Much depends upon proper selection of texts and materials and the development of well-ordered courses of study. Where several sections of a course exist, common examinations will do much to enforce adequate treatment of the various aspects of the program.

Applied music, or the study of performance, allows more freedom of choice to both instructors and students than does the theory-history program. Not only does the student choose which instruments he will study, but each performing organization will play a somewhat different role reflecting its unique potentialities and the approach of its director. Each music student enters the institution with previous experience as a singer or player on one or more instruments. This experience usually forms the basis for his choice of music as a vocation, and also provides him with an indispensable vehicle with which to develop his musical understanding. His most advanced performing medium thus becomes his "principal instrument," which he continues to study by means of regular private lessons, individual practice, and solo appearances, and which he employs as a member of one or more performing ensembles.

The student majoring in applied music, of course, must concentrate more of his effort in this particular area, since he expects to make his living as a performer. But the music composer, scholar, or educator also needs to achieve the highest possible level of performing ability; in this instance, his goal is not virtuosity, but the understanding of musical literature and the refinement of stylistic and interpretative abilities which will transfer to his vocation of musical composition, investigation, or teaching. The band director, for example, who has never performed adequately, literally cannot comprehend the full possibilities in a piece of music or properly coach his players in the best means to achieve them.

Curricular decisions are therefore in order regarding entrance requirements in performance, the choice of a field of applied study, credits to be required, repertoire to be studied and levels to be achieved, jury responsibilities, and recital performance and attendance requirements. Each teacher of applied music will possess his own standards and methodology, which may need to be somewhat adjusted to fit the objectives of the program and the individual needs of his students. For example, many teachers are preoccupied with the fundamentals of tone production and technique, so that their students are constantly assigned technical material to perfect their *ability* to perform. While this procedure is obviously necessary to some extent, and more so at certain times, the main job is to come to grips with musical literature.

In the students' secondary performing fields, on the other hand, the idea is to achieve basic technical understanding and functional ability. In most institutions, one or two years of piano and a term or two of voice are required of all music majors who are not already proficient in those fields, in the belief that basic functional skills in those areas are necessary tools in their future jobs. In addition, future teachers of instrumental music are ordinarily given exposure to several of the basic band and orchestral instruments through small classes meeting two or three periods per week.

As large a variety of performing organizations as possible should be sponsored by the university, since each possesses its unique literature and serves the needs of differing types of students. These may include the all-university chorus, select choirs, men's and women's choral ensembles, marching band, concert band, symphonic wind ensemble, percussion ensemble, brass choir, woodwind choir, stage band, symphony orchestra, chamber orchestra, baroque ensemble, collegium musicum, new music ensemble, opera workshop, music theatre company, and various small chamber groups of vocal and instrumental performers. The organizations to be supported in each institution will depend upon the resources of the music unit and the available manpower. Where numerous performing groups are established, care must be taken to ensure that weekly rehearsal times are adjusted to minimize conflicts, so that students may participate in more than one group. At the same time, it is necessary to avoid pressure upon the better students to participate in more groups than they can properly handle. Care must also be exercised to avoid abnormal weekly rehearsal time allotments to any of these organizations. More than three or four hours of rehearsal per week per credit will distort the curriculum and the students' individual programs of study.

Since the university director does not start his players and singers, or generally function as their individual teacher, he has less direct access to potential members than does his colleague in the schools. To secure a full and balanced group, therefore, he is often forced to the expedient of extensive recruitment measures and the use of scholarship funds as available. Furthermore, each director naturally tries to find the best performers to fill each section since places can usually be found for excess volunteers within some other organization. In order to staff the performing organizations with the least possible stress and strain, the benevolent assistance of the remaining music faculty is highly important. Each applied teacher, for example, needs to consider it part of his responsibility to help find needed performers to fill the section he represents; further, his assistance may be sorely needed to enhance the competence of that section by means of sectional rehearsals and/or individual coaching of its members. The director cannot properly handle his personnel problems without the aid of the entire music unit.

Within the allotted rehearsal time, the director must develop his organization into a functioning musical unit, acquaint the participants with appropriate musical literature, and prepare public presentations as seems most practicable. Like the directors of high school music organizations, his primary purpose must be to educate and not to entertain. But, because of the generally higher proficiency in college level organizations, the literature can usually be more advanced and the performance more sparkling. The director is *not* expected to select literature for training purposes, but rather should attempt to employ those numbers which are most characteristic for his medium and most practical for his group. With an advanced group, therefore, the literature may be highly advanced and *avant-garde;* much of it may never be employed by the members in their future jobs, yet it will serve best to promote their musical sensitivity and awareness.

Other courses in the undergraduate music curriculum include those specifically needed by future music teachers—instrumental and choral conducting, and methods and materials for teaching instrumental, choral, and general music in the elementary and secondary schools. These are normally coordinated with courses in the general historical and social foundations of education, school practice, and student teaching in music. The inherent problem lies, until student teaching is reached, in making the content of these courses applicable to school situations. That is, the conducting student may learn score reading and baton technique without learning how to rehearse live performers; the student may create a course of study in music for the elementary grades but never have a chance to see it put into operation. This problem obviously suggests measures to provide laboratory groups for the application of theories and principles developed in these classes. Student teaching, in its turn, absolutely requires careful provision of opportunities to observe and practice, under competent guidance, the complete range of instructional tasks that will be found on the job.

Graduate programs in music parallel the undergraduate programs. Normal specialties at the master degree level are in the various performing fields, music history and literature, music theory and composition, conducting, church music, and music education. Doctoral degrees are usually designated as:[3]

1. Doctor of Philosophy for creative scholarship and research in musicology, theory, music history and literature, or composition.
2. Doctor of Philosophy, Doctor of Education, or Doctor of Music Education for creative scholarship and research in music education.
3. Doctor of Musical Arts for performance or composition.
4. Doctor of Sacred Music or Doctor of Church Music for creative scholarship and performance in sacred music.

A new degree, the Doctor of Arts, has recently come upon the scene; it is deliberately geared toward the preparation of college and university teachers in any field, including music, rather than the production of researchers, composers, or performers.

For graduate degrees, requirements are usually carefully specified by an institution's own graduate school as to admission, residence, candidacy, language and tool requirements, thesis or project, committee selection, and final written and oral examinations. Course requirements for the individual programs, however, are normally broad and flexible. As

---

[3] See National Association of Schools of Music, *Graduate Studies* (Washington, D.C.: Bulletin 35 of the Association, 1968), p. 9.

with the undergraduate curriculum, administrative restraint needs to be exercised to preclude proliferation beyond legitimate demand and the institution's resources; there is no good end served by having outlined in the catalog a program that does not regularly produce graduates.

Too many graduate programs are cheap; to produce enrollments, any application is accepted, and the course offerings are limited and not truly advanced. While some excuse may be found for allowing every entering freshman to "try his hand," the same principle is not defensible at the graduate level. Graduate programs are too expensive and the result of low standards is too damaging to the profession. Accordingly, administrative provision must be made to secure highly qualified and specialized instructors of any graduate offerings. Admission must be restricted by reasonable examinations and grade averages. For adequate research, the music library holdings must be sufficiently extensive, and other specialized facilities such as an electronic music laboratory, a video tape machine, computer service, or a set of ancient instruments may need to be acquired for particular kinds of programs. Above all, every effort must be made to ensure that the courses are not mere extensions of undergraduate work; the course content at each level must be new and challenging to the students.

EXPEDITING INSTRUCTION

Within any educational institution, while the objectives of the music unit are being identified and the curriculum being established to achieve them, a parallel effort from the administration is needed to assist the instructors to accomplish their assigned responsibilities. This involves various coordinative and supportive activities. The purpose of the administration is to provide those services which will allow the instructors to concentrate upon their primary job of instruction.

SPACE AND EQUIPMENT

The first items which must be provided the instructor are office and teaching space and the basic equipment pertaining to his phase of the curriculum. Buildings and equipment will be treated extensively in a later chapter, but it should be pointed out here that it is a continuing administrative responsibility to maintain essential security of these facilities and to make certain that they are in usable condition. This state of affairs is achieved by means of regular physical plant maintenance and custodial services, coupled with upkeep of equipment through inventory, periodic inspection and renovation, repair and replacement as necessary. Rooms must be properly keyed and lockers provided as required. Insurance may be secured to protect against major loss. A system should be established for requesting and accomplishing equipment moves.

Where textbooks are not the responsibility of the individual student, a textbook service must be established. A system must be instituted for selecting, ordering, storing, distributing, and retrieving the textbooks.

Separate facilities are needed for filing and storing the scores and parts to be used by the various performing groups. Locations in or near the rehearsal hall are advisable, with plenty of working space for sorting music.

The music section of the school library needs regular attention. A stipulated portion of available funds should be reserved for the acquisition of music books and periodicals, and these must be catalogued and shelved. The library becomes a major item in colleges and universities, where the music curriculum demands considerable resources in terms of primary sources and reference material. The need is compounded where any significant graduate program exists. In some institutions it is found most practical to create a separate music library for the greater convenience of music students and faculty members; such an arrangement requires special provision of space for storage and study, and the services of a music librarian.

Audio/visual services are usually associated with the library. These services entail the regular acquisition of useful tapes and recordings, systematized filing and checkout, and multiple playback equipment. Playback facilities are also needed in each music classroom. Other audio/visual services may include slide projection, opaque projection, film projection, training aids, public address systems, portable and fixed recording facilities, videotape equipment, and closed circuit television. Necessary technical personnel must be at hand to operate and maintain this equipment.

CLASS SCHEDULING

Class scheduling is one of the major administrative responsibilities. There are several styles of class schedule. Informality is the rule in most elementary grades where, for example, the teacher may plan to work with the class on music daily from 10:00 to 10:20, following social studies, yet often is delayed and must postpone or skip the music session for that day. If the music class is to be taught by another classroom teacher or a music specialist, however, who appears at an appointed time, it becomes necessary to maintain the schedule; the same is true where the separate classes are brought on schedule to a special music room.

Where departmentalization occurs, usually in the secondary schools and colleges, the traditional schedule pattern involves assigning a room to each course for a certain number of periods per week. The process for any one term is as follows:

1. Determine the offerings and the weekly time allotment required for each course.

2. Estimate student demand for each course, the size and type of classroom needed, and the possible necessity for splitting into additional sections.

3. Make tentative assignment of instructors to the courses, based upon their qualifications and past assignment, and the rough equalization of their teaching loads. If loads prove to be too heavy, reduce by combining sections or by deleting courses which are considered optional. If loads prove to be too light, add further sections of large courses or add other courses which would appear attractive.

4. Prepare a master time schedule by distributing the courses among the time slots in the available teaching locations. Begin with the courses which require particular rooms, such as the large performing organizations. Try to distribute them evenly throughout the school day, avoiding time conflicts between those courses which would affect the same teachers and students. Secure official sanction for these room assignments as necessary.

5. Prepare the official class schedule which is to be printed or posted for registration purposes, listing course numbers and titles, credit, prerequisites, time and place, class size limits, and instructors.

Most secondary schools divide the school day into six 55-minute periods, or seven 45-minute periods, plus lunch periods and time for passing between classes. Modular scheduling is a device by which the day is divided into modules of fifteen or twenty minutes and each individual course and activity is allotted a certain number of modules per week. These may be arranged quite flexibly, so that the orchestra may use two consecutive modules on one day for string rehearsal and four modules on another day for rehearsal of the full orchestra. A number of the modules may also be on "open schedule," allowing the student to schedule this time among supervised study and private music lessons, independent study and practice, laboratory work and small musical ensemble rehearsals, special short courses, and conferences. Due to the complexity of this operation, students' programs are often arranged by use of a computer; such scheduling service is currently offered by Stanford University.

Even within the traditional pattern of fixed daily periods, certain music offerings will be superimposed upon that schedule by means of rotation and appointment. Individual lessons and groups of two or three are often scheduled by arrangement to meet during the students' free periods or study hours. Rotating periods are sometimes employed for small ensembles and sectional rehearsals, by scheduling each meeting at a different hour of the school day. The brass choir, for example, might be scheduled to meet on Tuesdays and Thursdays, beginning with the first period and moving to the next period on succeeding days. As illustrated below, the students would miss only one period every third week in any one of their regular classes:

Day and Period	M	T	W	Th	F	M	T	W	Th	F	M	T	W	Th	F
1		X													
2				X											
3							X								
4									X						
5												X			
6														X	

Some schools also employ "floating periods," whereby an activity period is reserved each day at a different hour. Clubs and all-school groups including musical organizations meet at these times:

	M	T	W	Th	F	M	T	W	Th	F
1	X						X			
2		X						X		
3			X						X	
4				X						X
5					X					
6						X				

STUDENT ADVISEMENT AND COUNSELING

Students regularly need advice regarding their programs of study, class assignments, career choice, and personal problems. All teachers do a certain amount of informal advising and counseling, but a corps of specialists in these fields is normally to be desired. These people need to know the institution's curriculum thoroughly and should have had special work in the field of counseling. Unfortunately, many general advisers and counselors do not really understand the special circumstances involved with the music curriculum nor do they comprehend the motivations of those students who are especially interested in the field of music. Hence they often give poor advice unless they can be carefully briefed by music personnel.

The problem occurs partially because music is ordinarily not required for college entrance. High school counselors are thus quite conscientious about setting up schedules for college-bound students to include the necessary "core" requirements; if a music course seems inconvenient to schedule, it is suggested that it can be dropped from the student's program. Unfortunately, this attitude tends to be accepted by other teachers, the students, and even their parents. The effects can be partially alleviated by contacting the student body directly, with prior administrative sanction, determining their individual intention to enroll in the various musical activities, and giving the counselors the class lists around which to build the students' programs.

Similar problems occur at the university level, where a general adviser cannot easily determine which instruments a music student needs to study and at which particular level he should begin. Neither can they accurately judge in which performing organization to enroll him. Unless such advisement can be arranged directly with music personnel, it is necessary to develop very specific instructions to the advisers.

Professional psychological counseling must be left to counselors trained in this field. But as far as career counseling for music goes, at any level, it would be best left to the students' music teachers. Only they can have sufficient knowledge of the students' musical potential and the necessary steps to be taken to prepare for a musical career.

ARRANGING PUBLIC EVENTS

Arrangements for mounting concerts, recitals, clinics, tours, and other special musical events is a large undertaking which demands careful administrative coordination. University music schools and many large public school music programs sponsor hundreds of such events during each school year. This process must be followed:

1. Each spring, working from the all-school calendar, the major musical events for the next season need to be determined. These will include all appearances by the large musical organizations, any tours, operas and musicals, and those concerts or clinics involving guest artists. Dates should be well spaced to give necessary rehearsal time, to avoid overworking students who may be involved in several events, and also to induce better attendance through better spacing of publicity. This process tends to be made easier by following traditional patterns that have proved most natural and practical. For example, the week before

Christmas may be held for the annual choral Christmas concert and the last week in April may be automatically reserved for the annual musical.

2. Halls must be booked for these appearances and for the necessary dress rehearsals. Adjustments will be needed when conflicts are found with other events which may have been already scheduled. All events must then be entered officially on the school calendar.

3. Less critical events such as solo recitals and small ensemble programs may then be scheduled and booked into the halls and entered on the calendar of the most convenient basis. Additional events of this type may be added throughout the year since only a month or two "lead time" is usually required.

4. For each event, it is necessary to determine some months in advance the equipment that will be required and its transport to and from the location must be arranged. Any needed music or equipment not on hand must be ordered.

5. As preparation for each event advances, a publicity campaign must be mounted. This will take the form of photographs and appropriate news copy released to the media. Advertisements and display posters may also be employed. Mailed invitations may be used, often in the form of yearly or quarterly mailing of the calendar of coming events.

6. If tickets are to be used, these must be printed and ticket sale arranged. Ushers and stagehands must be secured as required.

7. Standard procedure must be followed in arranging for students who must miss any classes for rehearsal or the final event.

8. Program copy must be prepared and sent to the printer; arrangements must be made for any recording or broadcast of the event.

9. Where visiting artists or clinicians are involved, arrangements will need to be made to meet them, and for their housing and entertainment. Preparation will be needed for any post-concert party or reception.

Many of the above responsibilities will fall upon the sponsoring teacher or his assistants, but administrative guidance will be required at several points. In many large institutions, the responsibility is delegated to News Service and Music Extension to assist directly with these matters.

Office Aids

Each music teacher needs access to numerous supplies and services which can best be performed or arranged by the central office of his music unit or of his school's principal. These include typing, copying, duplicating, mailing, telephone service, expendable supplies, requisition of equipment and physical plant services, and the keeping of inventories, student records, etc. As much as possible, these services should be available on a simple, routine basis, with a minimum of red tape.

All teachers need some supervision, even if only for the purpose of evaluating them. New teachers and those with less experience and expertise may need considerably more. As has been stated, this is a staff function of the lowest administrative echelon, to work with the teachers and their students toward improved instruction and thus to enhance the possibility of reaching the objectives of the school. The process has been treated extensively in several publications.[4] The effort is conducted by means of a combination of techniques: regular observation of instruction-in-progress, research, consultation, demonstrations, experimental programs, workshops, the development of courses of study and other teaching materials, and a continuing program of in-service education.

EVALUATION OF THE
MUSIC CURRICULUM

There are always three steps involved in evaluation: (1) identification of valid objectives, (2) the collection of pertinent data, and (3) interpretation of the data in terms of the objectives. Each instructor evaluates his individual students periodically on the basis of his stated or assumed objectives, in order to assign marks. Each faculty and staff member is likewise evaluated in terms of the discharge of his responsibilities for purposes of determining tenure, salary, and possible promotion. An educational institution as a whole, and its component parts, must also be evaluated in order to determine the extent to which it is fulfilling its proper role and to ascertain where desirable modifications can be made.

There are two aspects to the evaluation of an educational program. One has to do with the measurable achievement of its graduates as defined by the objectives of that program; the other deals with the relative condition of that institution to produce such results.

Most schools and colleges actually do a fair job on an informal basis, in evaluating their potential. The music administration and faculty, for example, generally have broad goals in mind and know pretty well what additional personnel, space, facilities, and programs they would like to see instituted to achieve them. This process is reinforced by the examinations provided by accrediting associations representing

---

4 See especially, Charles Leonhard and Robert W. House, *Foundations and Principles of Music Education,* 2nd ed. (New York: McGraw-Hill Book Company, 1972), chap. 10, and Keith D. Snyder, *School Music Administration and Supervision,* 2nd ed. (Boston: Allyn and Bacon, 1965), chap. 4.

specific regions and disciplines. At the university level, for example, these examinations are accomplished by the National Association of Schools of Music. Using criteria and procedures which are largely employed by all these agencies, their investigation covers fourteen points:[5]

I. *Music executive's load and responsibilities.* Is the music executive's load such that he has time and energy to execute effectively his administrative duties, and teaching responsibilities, if any? Are his responsibilities clearly delineated and understood, and is his authority commensurate with his responsibility?

II. *Policy-making.* How is curricular and educational policy established? To what extent is the faculty involved? Consider the general characteristics of the institution, and the specific practices in the music unit. Compare your impressions with the response to question 6 of the self-survey.

III. *Objectives.* The examiner should note any inappropriate objectives, or any discrepancies between the stated objectives and the examiner's impression of what the actual objectives are.

IV. *Degrees and curricula in operation.* This section should give comparisons with NASM criteria for similar curricula, as well as the examiner's judgment of the effectiveness of these curricula in relation to the stated objectives. Any significant departures from common practice should be noted and evaluated.

V. *Study of the transcripts of recent graduates* (see question 12a of the self-survey) and comparison with catalogue statements. Any significant discrepancies should be noted.

VI. *Enrollment.* If the information in the self-survey does not cover the breakdown for the academic year in which the visitation is made, please secure it and include in your report.

VII. *Admission and retention.* Report on admission and retention policies and procedures of the institution generally and of the music unit specifically, and of the quality of institution-wide record keeping.

VIII. *Evaluation of students' work.* Summarize your observations on the quality of work in applied music; class courses in theory, music history and literature, music education, including practice teaching and methods courses.

IX. *Student body.* Summarize impressions regarding competence, morale, and level of accomplishment.

X. *Training and competence of the faculty,* based on study of the faculty report forms; evaluation of their teaching, based on class visitations, auditions, and conferences.

XI. *Teaching loads of faculty.* Report any special observations on faculty teaching loads. Does the self-survey, questions 25–26–27, accurately represent the faculty load situation in the music unit? What is the faculty morale?

---

[5] National Association of Schools of Music, *Instructions for Examiners,* unpublished pamphlet, One Dupont Circle, Washington, D.C.

XII. *Physical plant and equipment.* Is it adequate in terms of space, practice facilities, sound control, audio equipment, lighting, temperature and humidity control, instruments, maintenance, etc.?

XIII. *Library:* Books, scores, recordings, multiple copies of ensemble music. Evaluate holdings in relation to what is normally needed for the curricula offered. Are the annual appropriations for the library adequate? Is library equipment such as phonographs, microfilm or microcard readers, etc. accessible and adequate?

XIV. *Summary* of strengths and weaknesses of the music program. The examiner should include constructive suggestions for future development, based on the observations reported above. *This summary is the most important single contribution the examiner can make to the visited institution.*

Any institution may proceed with a self-survey at any time, using the above format. However, it will be noted that the main thrust in such an examination is necessarily upon observation of the current operation; the idea is to determine to what extent the institution is *capable* of accomplishing what it is trying to do. But the only valid measure of accomplishment is the *degree of progress* of the students toward the objectives, over a period of time. Unless this can be estimated, an institution with a highly selected student body will always seem more successful than one whose students start nearer the bottom. For a complete evaluation, it is necessary to secure a measure of the musicianship and careers of the graduates as compared with the status of the incoming students.

The music administrator therefore needs to supplement the informal judgment of the music faculty and the periodic examinations by accrediting bodies with a sustained effort to discover whether the music curriculum is effective. A systematic testing program is required. It is also important to maintain contact with the graduates of the institution to determine whether they are still applying the musicianship they acquired there. What portion remain with music as a vocation and how notable have they become? How many continue to participate actively in music as an avocation? Do they support musical events with their attendance? Do they possess good recordings and listen to good musical broadcasts? Are their children participating in music? Such answers are difficult to come by, but they supply the true measure of the music curriculum and provide the key to any profitable revisions of it.

QUESTIONS FOR DISCUSSION

1. What is the curriculum and why is it of vital concern to the administration?

2. Why are objectives at the root of curriculum formation? How

is it that all music programs are so similar in outline and pursue the same broad goals, yet must create their own set of objectives? Describe the different levels of objectives and how they must relate in forming the basis for the curriculum. What can the administrator do to further the development of useful objectives?

3. What are the major divisions of the music program in elementary schools, and how do these naturally extend and proliferate into the secondary school music program? What kind of music program does the administrator wish to encourage and how does he go about it?

4. Describe the general and vocational offerings in music normally found in university undergraduate and graduate programs. What are some of the problems in designing and conducting these activities which should be of administrative concern?

5. What is the administrative role in providing the space and equipment for instruction? What is involved in maintaining these items and making them available for use?

6. Review the process involved in developing a workable schedule of classes. What are the mechanisms of the rotating schedule and the modular schedule?

7. What are some of the ways and means of securing effective advisement and counseling of music students?

8. Why is the preparation of the music calendar so complex and critical to the smooth working of the curriculum? What procedures are involved?

9. What is the value of deliberate evaluation of the music program? Who and what are to be evaluated, and for what purposes? What processes are followed? Why is it important to make the distinction between a music unit's capabilities and its actual outcomes?

SUGGESTED READINGS

Bruner, Jerome S., *The Process of Education*. Cambridge, Mass.: Harvard University Press, 1961.

Evaluative Criteria. Washington, D.C.: National Study of Secondary School Evaluation, 1960.

Goodland, John I, and Robert H. Anderson, *The Nongraded Elementary School*. New York: Harcourt Brace Jovanovich, 1959.

Hoffer, Charles K., *Teaching Music in the Secondary Schools.* Belmont, California: Wadsworth Publishing Co., Inc., 1965.

Leonhard, Charles, and Robert W. House, *Foundations and Principles of Music Education,* 2nd ed. New York: McGraw-Hill Book Company, Inc., 1972, chaps. 6, 7, 11.

Moses, Harry E., *Developing and Administering a Comprehensive High School Music Program.* West Nyack, N.Y.: Parker Publishing Co., 1970.

Salor, J. Galen, and William M. Alexander, *Curriculum Planning for Modern Schools.* New York: Holt, Rinehart & Winston, Inc., 1966.

Snyder, Keith D., *School Music Administration and Supervision,* 2nd ed. Boston: Allyn and Bacon, Inc., 1965.

CHAPTER FOUR

music faculty development

It is a truism that one can only teach what he knows. This belief is sometimes wrongly interpreted to mean, for example, that one cannot successfully teach an instrument unless he plays it. Actually, it is entirely possible for a good performer to do so, by extrapolating principles of tone production, technique, and musical style from his own instrument to the requirements of another. It is done all the time. And the successful director of a band can often do quite well with orchestras and choirs. It is really a matter of being a successful person and teacher, plus possession of a working concept of what needs to be taught.

A primary administrative goal, therefore, is to provide each sector of the curriculum with the individual faculty member or members who can actually produce the desired outcomes. It is obvious that the correlation will be very high between the quality of faculty and the results that obtain.

Equally important will be the ability of those faculty members to work together as a team. There is value in having individuals of different types—planners, experimenters, organizers, questioners, perfectionists, showmen, and doers—so long as each plays his part constructively. A competent, well-adjusted faculty generates its own directions with a minimum of supervision and mediation.

This chapter will deal with the recruitment and selection of music faculty. It will also cover other aspects of their employment, such as contracts, collateral benefits, assignments, and evaluation for salary, tenure, and promotion. Procedure will be discussed for creating effective working conditions and enhancing their good partnership in the educational enterprise.

FACULTY RECRUITMENT
AND SELECTION

Faculties are seldom created *en masse*. A faculty position which is to be filled is normally the result of retirement, resignation, or an authorized expansion, and the type of individual to be sought depends upon the particular slot that needs to be filled. Thus, when the choral director resigns, a new choral director must be found to assume those duties. If a second position is to be created in the choral area, a somewhat different combination of talents is sought in order that the two individuals may divide the work in the most expeditious way.

Even when a single replacement is sought, however, every possibility should be explored for strengthening the faculty. The evolving curriculum may point to the need for a different emphasis in this faculty position. Thus, it may become feasible to replace the retiring orchestra director with one who is also an active violinist or cellist, in order to build toward a faculty string quartet; the resignation of the choral director may enable the shift which was desired toward music theatre, by procuring a younger and more enterprising instructor with experience in both choral and theatrical work.

Over the years, the recruitment and selection of music faculty should be conducted on the basis of deliberate policy. This policy should always be concerned with the overall profile of the faculty which is to be achieved some five or ten years in the future. If the policy is effective, the faculty will gradually evolve into a well-balanced instrument for achieving the curriculum. Not only will each sector of the curriculum be properly manned, but there will be a balance of experience and youth. There will be a proper diversity of talent and philosophy. Perhaps there will be a few faculty members who were among the most brilliant and promising products of the institution itself, but excessive inbreeding will be carefully avoided.

JOB DESCRIPTION

Having these points in mind, it is necessary to have a job description prepared. This is ordinarily a cooperative task involving those who must work most directly with the new instructor—his immediate colleagues and supervisor. Only they can determine the specific functions he must perform and the kind of background needed to perform them. Once administrative clearance is obtained to proceed on this basis, a position notice is prepared, which condenses the job description and adds other information necessary to the candidates. The position notice defines (1) the nature of the position, (2) the job to be done, (3) the qualifications desired, (4) the conditions of employment, and (5) the nature of the institution and the community.

The good position notice is specific but not too exclusive. If the notice specifies theorist, oboist, male, Ph.D., the applications will be rather restricted and a weaker teacher may result than if a more flexible notice is given. One never knows what desirable combination of talents he may discover. He may be seeking a musicologist and find one who is also a harpist!

A typical position notice is as follows:

Music position at Northern State College

for an Instructor or Assistant Professor of Brass Instruments

to teach individual and class lessons on trombone, baritone, and tuba, and to organize and coach small brass ensembles and/or stage band.

Candidate must possess master's degree and successful experience as a teacher of the lower brass instruments. Performing ability desirable.

Salary: $9–12,000 per academic year, depending upon degrees and experience. Summers extra. Duties begin next September 1st.

Northern State is a college enrolling some 5,000 students. There are about one hundred undergraduate music majors, mostly in music education, and a music faculty of twelve. The college is located in the city of Fairmont, pop. 8,000, surrounded by mountains and many recreational facilities.

Candidates should send a tape of their playing and have placement credentials forwarded. Make application directly to John Doe, Chairman, Department of Music, phone (268) 318–4000.

ADVERTISING THE OPENING

Institutions advertise open positions by a number of means and usually contact several sources. Ideally, the need for a teacher is known by midwinter, so there are several months to do a thorough canvass before contracts are signed and releases become difficult to obtain. Elementary and secondary schools tend to rely upon personal contacts and nearby university placement services, since their candidates must be certified by the state office of education. Some of these schools, however, and most institutions of higher learning, go further afield. In this case, the notice will be sent to several of the large university placement bureaus, and perhaps to one or two of the commercial teachers agencies, and interviews may be arranged at national meetings of the professional associations. A popular and productive device in recent years has been to circularize the member institutions of the National Association of Schools of Music. An even more direct approach has been to send notices to the names categorized by field of specialization in the *Directory of Music Faculties,* published by the College Music Society. And a favorite method has always been to call or write personal acquaintances who may be interested or who are in a position to know of likely candidates. Sometimes an individual has already been observed on the job and is felt to be a likely candidate. Most institutions also retain files on applications received without solicitation, and these may be consulted when a particular opening occurs.

The job of finding qualified applicants has recently become easier with the so-called saturation of the teaching market. It is true that the total number of available teachers has come to exceed total demand, yet there are still shortages of really qualified personnel for particular kinds of jobs.

SCREENING APPLICANTS

If a thorough job of advertising an opening has been done, numerous applications will follow. These must be systematically acknowledged and collected, and notes kept on any telephoned applications or field interviews. These data need to be reviewed by a screening committee representing the administrative and teaching personnel who originally prepared the job description. Their job is to narrow the applications to the two or three who most nearly fit the need of the institution. This is done by carefully combing the applicants' letters, vita sheets, transcripts, concert programs, tapes, and recommendations to discover their true qualifications and by matching these with the committee's picture of the ideal candidate. At least one of the screening committee needs to be experienced in this process, for much important information is below the surface and received by inference. This is because the candidate is selling himself and because recommendations are almost invariably kind. It is usually wise to conduct a very careful reevaluation of data relating to the top candidates, to discover any gaps in information or suspected areas of weakness. Where doubts persist, questions should be raised directly with the candidates or their close associates.

When the selection is finally completed, the recommendations of the screening committee are presented to the hiring authority in whose name the notice went out. He must weigh the nominees very carefully and determine whether one should be offered the job or, as is usually the case, be invited for an interview. If he does not see any candidate matching the needs of the job, he should require that the process of advertising and screening be continued.

INTERVIEW

Sometimes two or three candidates are invited for interview, but it is usually best to begin with the most likely candidate and make him the offer if he proves to be as expected. The interview is confirmatory. It is properly done at the institution's expense unless the offer is made and refused without adequate reason.

The visit should be made when school is in session and the candidate may see the music program in operation. He should have opportunity to visit with those faculty members who would become his immediate colleagues and with administrative officials with whom he would be working. He must be auditioned if musical performance is to be an aspect of his job. He should inspect the physical plant and equipment with which he would be dealing. Procedural details and personnel policies should be reviewed. He should procure information describing fringe benefits such as sick leave, sabbaticals, group hospitalization, life insurance, and retirement plan. His purpose is to determine whether this is the kind of situation in which he can successfully operate and to compare it with his present position.

Those whom he contacts will learn much from his questions and his bearing. They will be looking for any item which does not square with the picture they had of him from his credentials. They will be measuring him against the requirements of the job and assessing their own ability to work with him as a colleague.

The opinions of all who observed the candidate should be made available to the hiring official as soon as possible. Sometimes this can be done within hours and sometimes it will take days. Sometimes the opinions will be conflicting. But this person must decide on the basis of all available judgment whether or not an offer is to be made, and if so, the quicker the better.

THE OFFER

Where there is a single salary schedule the offer tends to be cut and dried, since the candidate already knows what his salary and duties will be; any bargaining usually revolves around the promise of certain needed equipment, assisting personnel, summer employment, or changes in direction of the program. But where rank and salary are negotiable, as in most colleges, the institution must find the offer which is sufficient to attract the candidate without going beyond the rank and salary of those on the staff with equivalent qualifications. This offer must be communicated to the candidate together with any special agreement regarding moving expenses, summer employment, and the like. A contract should be signed or a notice of appointment mailed and accepted in writing.

If the offer is not accepted or rejected immediately, no more than forty-eight hours should be allowed for consideration; usually, longer delay means that the candidate is awaiting an offer from another institution or bargaining for a higher salary in his present position. In any case, it is necessary to proceed with the search without further delay.

ASSIGNMENT

The initial assignment of responsibilities has been made with the offer and acceptance of appointment. But it is necessary to develop specific load assignments based upon the principle of equalized loads. It is true that many teachers will do as little as possible to cover their assignment, while others will cheerfully put in twice the required time and effort. But the assigned teaching load must be based upon averages or probabilities.

Teaching loads are assigned on the principle that the teacher will need to spend about forty hours per week to accomplish his tasks. That is, the assigned classes are weighted in terms of the outside time needed for preparation and follow up. A kindergarten teacher, for example, may be working with her class only fifteen hours per week, but must spend more time than that in preparing for class. The instructor of music theory, like an English composition teacher, usually devotes at least twice as much time in correcting papers as he spends in class. The band director consumes countless hours in preparing marching evolutions and in managing the instruments and equipment pertaining to his organization. The guidance of theses and student research projects, student teacher supervision, student conferences and advisement, committee assignments, and administrative duties are among the special tasks that need to be taken into account in assigning loads.

Research and writing, musical composition, and performance are importance adjuncts of instruction, especially at the university level; these are among the contributions which advanced educational institutions are supposed to make to society. Qualified music personnel are thus often assigned part of their loads in such areas, as artists or composers in residence. Needless to say, tangible results must be expected from any such assignment.

The following formula is a general guide in determining loads, although adjustments are in order to allow for extra large classes, assigned administrative responsibilities, the availability of help from student assistants and office personnel, etc.:

Elementary and secondary schools	*Full load (hrs per wk.)*
large performing organizations	15
lecture courses	20
small ensembles and sectionals, class and individual lessons	25
College and university	
lecture courses	12
large performing organizations	12
individual lessons in performance or composition	18 (or 36 half hours)
class lessons, drill sessions, small ensembles	24
research, composition, performance	40
student teaching supervision, thesis guidance, etc.	36 students

ORIENTATION

New faculty members are specially in need of administrative guidance in approaching their duties. This concern extends to acquainting them with the community, the faculty and students, and procedures of the institution. When a new faculty member is appointed, he should be made aware of the regulations and options available to him on professional memberships, sabbatical leave, sick leave, allowances for travel and study, life and hospital insurance, and retirement plans. He will need to know how his yearly salary is to be divided and paid, and the deductions that may be involved. He should understand policy on salary raises, tenure, promotion, and transfer. He should know to whom he is directly responsible and whom else he will need to approach for other decisions and assistance in discharging his responsibilities.

The new faculty member will be especially concerned about housing. He will usually appreciate being given any leads on available housing, including the names of reliable realtors. He may also wish to know about the local doctors and dentists, and about the schools his children will be attending. He must not be overlooked in issuing invitations to general social gatherings, meetings of local service clubs, and state and local professional meetings.

It is most important that the new faculty member be made acquainted with his students and faculty colleagues. He will need to be introduced at the first faculty meeting and given opportunity for extended conversations with his immediate associates. If he will direct a performing organization, he may appreciate being put in contact with student leaders in that group before school opens, for better transition into his duties. He should be introduced, or at least announced, to any student assembly held during the opening days of school.

Adequate notice of his appointment should be released to local news media and especially to the school paper.

Administrative concern for the new faculty member should extend beyond the first weeks of his tenure. A short, discreet visit to one or two of his classes is in order, and attendance at his first concert program is mandatory in order to demonstrate interest and support; such early visits also provide excellent opportunity for constructive advice. Initial, informal evaluations by administrators often help set the course for teachers for years to come.

FACULTY COMMUNICATION
AND MORALE

The individual faculty member works on two planes—as one discharging his direct instructional duties and also as one dealing with other faculty members and administrative officials who are likewise concerned with his students. His instructional job is necessarily affected by his perception of the work and beliefs of his colleagues and by his ability to coordinate his efforts with theirs. Thus, it becomes a definite administrative responsibility to see to the communication among faculty members and their morale.

To insure proper communications, faculty members need to understand the formal and informal structure of the organization. That is, they should know their location within the faculty organization and how their responsibilities relate to those of their colleagues. The band and orchestra directors, for example, need to understand how wind and percussion players are to be assigned and transferred between their organizations, and all cooperating directors need to know how the joint musical productions are to be managed and staffed. Applied music teachers should be aware of their responsibilities and prerogatives regarding the performing organizations. All music teachers need to understand how special equipment and services are procured. Coordinative responsibilities and committee assignments need to be clarified.

A thorough faculty handbook is an excellent device for avoiding confusion on standard policies and routine procedures. The range of such items is illustrated by the following index to one such publication:

Faculty Handbook
Index

	Page
Absence from Campus	17
Advisement and Registration	22
Answers to Student Questions	22
Application for Admission	22
Approval of Overloads	24
Change of Grade Card	25
Closed Class Requests	24
Completion of Registration	24
Concert and Recital Scheduling	21
Concerto Auditions	13
Current Advisory Committee Assignments	6
Equipment	14
Faculty Appointments	15
Faculty Committee Assignments	5
Faculty Travel	19
Financial Assistance	12
Flowers	21
General Policy for Performing Organizations	9
Graduation Checks	25
Housing	22
Jury Procedures	7
Listening Room	19
Major Ensembles	23
Objectives	2
Office Schedules	20
Operating Papers	3
Outside Employment	17
Performance Requirements for Graduation	8
Phones	14

	Page
Piano Accompanying	15
Policy on Supply of Wind and Percussion Players	10
Presser Awards	12
Proficiency Forms	25
Promotions in Rank	18
Publicity	10
Rehearsals	10
Research Grants	16
Restricted Class Cards	24
Sabbaticals	18
Salaries	18
Scheduling of Rooms	20
School of Music General Performance Policy	8
Student Teaching	25
Studio Hours	17
Summer Employment	16
Summer Workshops	21
Taping Concerts	20
Teaching Assignments	16
Tenure	18
Tours	11
Transfer from Another Institution	24
Transfer from General Studies to Music	24
Typing and Duplicating	19
Use of Harpsichord	26
Video Tape	20
Work Block	25
Xerox Machine	26

Most importantly, each member of the faculty needs ready access to his immediate superior and other administrative personnel with whom he must work. An easy working relationship must be established. Only in this way will mutual confidence be established and opportunity provided for smoother and more effective operations.

Good communication also relates to the mechanism for relaying information and news. Faculty mailboxes should be centrally located for relaying memos and other messages. Committee reports, administrative plans, and pertinent data need to be regularly circulated. A well-planned intercom or telephone system needs to be established. Faculty meetings must be held frequently enough to discharge essential business and to allow debate on significant issues.

In short, the administrator is obliged to encourage the kind of climate wherein the members of his unit communicate freely in the solution of problems and will acquire sympathetic appreciation of the tasks and activities of their colleagues. A sense of community among the music faculty is imperative. Any faculty member who does not respond to generous treatment, but reacts instead in a selfish, imperious manner, will disrupt the operation and should become a special concern; such a person, even though he may be unusually competent in his own tasks, cannot be allowed to continue as an impediment to the organization.

Good communication is only one aspect in achieving the faculty morale which supports effective teamwork. This point was mentioned briefly at the end of Chapter Two. Good morale results from the perception of progress toward goals. Hence, the music faculty members must *want* to produce more and finer music students, and then be given the kinds of assignments that they can work at effectively. Next, they must be shown the ways and provided the means to accomplish their tasks as a united and effective team. Finally, their individual work needs to be fairly evaluated and interpreted for them and properly rewarded with appropriate security, recognition, and status. This process provides the impetus for their further effort.

EVALUATION

We have just pointed out the crucial importance of evaluation in faculty development. One purpose of the evaluation is diagnostic. Since student progress is the true measure of teaching success, it becomes necessary to relate the work of the teacher to the objectives he is expected to accomplish—that is, to the kinds of musicianship he is supposed to be developing in his pupils, in keeping with the kinds of pupils he has to work with and the resources he has to command in his task. On that basis, he may be judged relatively successful or unsuccessful.

Techniques for evaluation are difficult in an educational setting, since an accurate estimate of student behavior is hard to achieve. It is even more difficult to determine the exact causes of deficient achievement by the students. What musical progress have the students made, what has caused it, and what might have been done to improve it?

Attempts have been made to secure a measure of musical achievement by standardized tests such as the Graduate Record Examination.[1] In order to measure progress, however, such tests will need to be given before and after the students' period of study. There are several other tests which can be given to measure particular facets of musical behavior.[2] But these are often ponderous to administer, score, and interpret, and often do not secure the specific information needed. Locally constructed tests are usually more useful. In addition, the problem occurs in that measurable knowledge and skill are only a part of the musical behaviors that are sought; pupil attitudes, appreciation, and habits must be inferred from observation of their regular musical activity.

One seemingly reliable measure of achievement lies in the excellence of public performance, particularly when submitted to adjudication at a music contest. But most music teachers recognize that any one public performance displays only a fraction of the repertoire, which has been subjected to detailed study and drill, and hardly tells what lasting musical behavior may result.

If it is difficult to determine student progress, it is even harder to determine what the teachers' role has been. A check on their planned courses of study will reveal much, but does not guarantee how the material will be presented. Periodic observation of their instruction is also unreliable, since some good teachers "freeze" and others will exert special effort and charm on such occasions which they may not employ on a daily basis. Neither are polls of their students entirely reliable, since personality and prejudice often count for more with them than solid teaching procedure; the most popular teacher is not necessarily the best one. Reports by their fellow faculty members are not to be entirely trusted either, since these colleagues are more affected by their compatibility than by their teaching ability.

None of the techniques outlined above provides a completely reliable index to a teacher's impact upon his students. But taken altogether they begin to add up to a convincing profile. If one's courses are well planned and the classes and rehearsals seem to be alive and stimulating, if his students do well enough on examinations and recitals, if his organizations are growing and performing well, if he follows through on assignments, and if opinions of his students and colleagues are favorable, then this teacher is obviously an asset to the school. Where the

---

1 Educational Testing Service, Princeton, N.J.

2 James Aliferis, *Aliferis Musical Achievement Test*, University of Minnesota Press, Minneapolis, 1954; Stephen E. Farnum, *Farnum Music Notation Test*, The Psychological Corporation, New York, 1953; William E. Knuth, *Knuth Achievement Tests in Music*, Educational Test Bureau, Inc., Philadelphia; John G. Watkins and Stephen E. Farnum, *Watkins-Farnum Performance Scale for All Band Instruments*, Hal Leonard Music, Inc., Winona, Minn., 1954.

opposite is the case, the results will usually indicate the cause or causes. These may include insufficient faculty and administrative support, inadequate musicianship, lack of knowledge and experience, ineffective personality, lack of planning, personal problems, or sheer lack of drive. Appropriate remedial action might include discreet advice and counsel toward improved methods or approach, or more help and resources to do the job. Sometimes a shift in assignment appears to be a more promising solution, while very occasionally it becomes advisable to seek a teacher's dismissal.

The evaluative process that we have described is continuous and necessarily qualitative. It is hazardous and there are many who believe that it should not be attempted since no one can accurately measure a teacher's success in the performance of his duties. Yet not to make the attempt is the more dangerous course. An occasional well-meaning mistake is preferable to the complete abdication of this responsibility. For how else is a faculty to be improved, and how else can judgment be made on salary raises, tenure, and promotion?

The single salary schedule employed by most elementary and secondary school systems is based entirely upon the individual's attainment of degrees and teaching experience. It is generally designed so that the beginning salary for one possessing a bachelor's degree and no experience will be approximately doubled, through yearly increments, after fifteen years' service and completion of the master's degree. A large additional amount normally accrues through cost of living increases and the consequent improvement of the basic minimums and maximums.

The single salary schedule is a result of the conclusion that a fair evaluation of teachers cannot be made. It is a pernicious policy, largely promoted by teachers associations and unions to enable them to deliver an attractive package contract. For a dubious security, the teachers who have supported the policy have traded the chance to be judged on their merit. The result is that individual brilliance and enterprise are discounted; mediocrity is rewarded.

Another damaging aspect of the single salary schedule is that it makes no allowance for the law of supply and demand. At certain times and places different teaching posts are harder to supply. For example, it may be necessary to pay a physics teacher more than an English teacher, in order to acquire and hold him. A qualified musicologist may demand more salary than an equally qualified choral director. To deny this fact only leads to an unbalanced faculty and a siphoning off of unique types to those institutions who will pay for what they must have.

In schools and colleges where salary raises are determined on the basis of merit plus cost of living increase, there is a chance to attract and retain stronger faculty members. In order to do this, evaluative records

are kept and reviewed yearly at the time salary raises must be recommended. Reserving a certain percentage for any cost of living increase,
the remaining percentage is divided according to the merit rating of each
teacher. This is determined by judging his relative performance of
duties, and estimating the difficulty of finding a similarly qualified replacement. In short, the largest raises go to those whose loss would be
most keenly felt.

Some schools have attempted to retain their salary schedule while
partially remedying its defects by means of special increments for special
responsibilities such as coaching, directing musical organizations, etc.
These posts are also often placed on a twelve-month rather than on the
nine-month basis. But the basic lack of incentive remains, in that raises
are automatic and not earned. Some schools have gone one step further
by establishing a ceiling upon automatic increments, and allowing for
"super maximums." Although these measures have value, tinkering with
the mechanism of salary schedules is no true substitute for a flexible
system based upon merit.

Promotion in rank is another incentive in university circles. Four
basic ranks exist:

1. The *Instructor* is a beginning teacher possessing the minimum degree
   required by the institution for such a post—usually a master's degree.
   To secure promotion to the next rank, he is ordinarily expected to
   show evidence of successful teaching during the next five or six years,
   and to secure an additional degree.
2. The *Assistant Professor* is the basic rank for teachers with successful
   teaching experience and advanced degrees. It does not relate to professional stature based upon professional activity, publication, and
   creative work. Hence, many fine teachers are not promoted from this
   rank.
3. The *Associate Professor* is one who has discharged his teaching responsibilities well over a considerable period of time and, in addition, has
   made authentic contributions to his discipline. He is recognized in and
   beyond his institution as an author, researcher, composer, or performer
   of stature, and is active in professional circles.
4. The *Professor* is one who has continued his professional contributions
   until he is a recognized authority in his particular field. Certain professors may also be designated as "research professor," or "distinguished
   professor."

In addition to the above, many institutions also employ the title of
Lecturer to designate one who is appointed for a limited time, and often
on a part-time basis. It is essentially a temporary rank, usually considered below that of Instructor but often paid at a higher rate. Some institutions also employ the rank of Assistant Instructor to indicate a sort of
internship arrangement.

It may be seen that there is a relationship between rank and salary, but it is not normally fixed. That is, there are overlapping ranges, so that the long-time assistant professor who is an excellent teacher and is extremely valuable to the institution may have a higher salary than the associate professor who has achieved his rank largely as a result of his added degrees and publications. The relationship between rank and salary stems from the fact that the determinant of salary—value to the institution—partially correlates with the determinant of rank—professional stature.

Selection of candidates for promotion is complicated by the fact that control is usually exercised by the institution to maintain a rough balance among the four ranks. This policy limits the number that can be promoted and forces comparison of the records of those who are recommended. This fact, in turn, easily produces misunderstanding among those whose promotion is long delayed, unless measures are taken to clarify promotional policy and procedure. If the system is to work properly in encouraging productivity, it is important to resist personal pressures and to maintain a legitimate basis for all promotion recommendations.

Selection for administrative posts is usually not considered promotion in university circles, but rather is viewed as a transfer in assignment. Rank is permanent and is usually retained when moving to another institution, but administrative assignment may be withdrawn at any time. Since the elementary and secondary schools do not use the system of professorial rank, however, administrative assignments tend to be regarded as promotions. Selection for administrative assignment at any level has little relation to qualification for rank; instead, ability to discharge the responsibilities as defined in our first and second chapters is the prime consideration.

It is regrettable that the elementary and secondary schools have not adopted a system of professorial ranks. The establishment of ranks such as teaching intern, instructor, senior instructor, and master teacher would go far to remedy the defects of the single salary schedule so long as the promotions are to be earned rather than automatic.

Academic tenure is also related to rank and experience, being designed to protect the teacher who has already demonstrated his value and competence from loss of his position due to biased or capricious judgment. Tenure laws protecting public school teachers have been enacted in most states and are observed by most universities. They provide that, after tenure is granted following the required probationary period, one may not be dismissed except "for cause." Three years is the usual probationary period in the public schools, and in universities it is normally five years for instructors, four years for assistant professors, two years for associate professors, and one year for professors. An additional year's notice of dismissal is also required when tenure is not granted.

Dismissal for cause is usually defined by statute or regulation to include financial exigency, cutbacks in program, immoral or unprofessional conduct, dishonesty, incompetence, unfitness for service, willful neglect of duty, physical or mental condition making one unfit to associate with students, persistent violation of school laws and regulations, and conviction of a felony. Such charges must be proved in open hearing. Such action is difficult to undertake and is usually quite disruptive to the school's operation. Hence, tenure laws often have the effect of protecting those whom the institution feels are incompetent.

The obvious answer to this problem is to employ extreme care in granting tenure. Only those who have actually proved during the period of probation that they are competent teachers and good working colleagues should be approved. No charges or proof of incompetence or incompatibility are required in order to give notice of dismissal before tenure is achieved. When there is substantial doubt, therefore, it is better to give the required notice of dismissal and make the search for a replacement. Administrators who duck this responsibility often live to regret it.

When tenure has been unwisely granted, and when formal charges do not seem expedient, the obvious recourse is to encourage the faculty member to leave through minimal salary raises or by reassignment to a post where his shortcomings are not so damaging. Some institutions have relieved themselves of an unwanted faculty member by negative response to his requests for support of his phase of the instructional program. Such action is not recommended, for it wrecks the program and penalizes the students in order to secure the resignation.

All these difficulties in dealing with faculty who have been unwisely retained points up the fact that faculty evaluations must be carefully done and all data recorded, as means to the best decisions on tenure, salary raises, and promotion. Faculty committees on promotion and tenure are often of great assistance in reviewing faculty and making recommendations on these matters.

The result of a sustained effort at music faculty development will be a well-selected faculty, properly assigned, confirmed in their competence, and working together wholeheartedly toward the achievement of valid curricular objectives. If this is successfully done, the remainder of the administrative task becomes relatively easy to accomplish.

QUESTIONS FOR DISCUSSION

1. Why does effective faculty development require long-term planing? What must the administrator have in mind when he is seeking a faculty addition or replacement?

2. What are the necessary ingredients of a practical job description? How is it developed? How is it advertised?

3. Describe the screening process, the interview, and offer of employment.

4. On what bases are teaching assignments made and loads determined? What is involved in proper orientation and guidance of the new faculty member?

5. How may administrators contribute to better communication and morale of the faculty?

6. What are some techniques for measuring a faculty member's effectiveness and why are these so difficult to apply? What are the uses of such evaluation?

7. Compare the practicality of the single salary schedule and the merit raise policy. What criteria are most appropriate for determining merit raises? What is the relationship to promotion in rank?

8. What factors need to be considered in recommending tenure?

SUGGESTED READINGS

Castetter, William B., *The Personnel Function in Educational Administration.* New York: The Macmillan Company, 1971.

Davis, Donald E., and Neal C. Nickerson, Jr., *Critical Issues in School Personnel Administration.* Chicago: Rand McNally and Co., 1968.

Donovan, J. J., ed., *Recruitment and Selection in the Public Service.* Chicago: Public Personnel Association, 1968.

Fawcett, Claude W., *School Personnel Administration.* New York: The Macmillan Company, 1964.

Redfern, George B., *How to Appraise Teaching Performance.* Columbus, Ohio: School Management Institute, Inc., 1965.

Savage, William W., *Interpersonal and Group Relations in Educational Administration.* Glenview, Ill.: Scott, Foresman & Co., 1968.

CHAPTER FIVE

working with music students

Since the essential product of any educational program consists of the improved competence of its graduates, the administration is necessarily involved in overseeing the activities of the students and establishing the best possible conditions for their instruction. Many administrators operate at a distance from the students on the assumption that administrators must work with the faculty and the faculty in turn works with the students. This is a mistake, for the administrator needs student input and the students deserve the guidance and regulation that only the administration can provide. This chapter deals with the characteristics of the student body, their needs and attitudes, and their advisement and counseling. It also discusses their recruitment and placement in the music program and the provision of resources for their use. Finally, it covers measures affecting student communication and morale, the promotion of their scholarship and musicianship, and the evaluation and reporting of their progress.

THE STUDENT POPULATION

Today's students have been characterized as more knowledgeable and independent than any in the past. If this is so, it is because of the explosion of knowledge and the improved methodology of instruction. Although many exceptions can be found, students at all levels are being given greater access to valid, useful information and a freer hand in exploring it than was formerly the case.

At the same time, schooling has become more universal. That is, more students are in school during a longer period of years. More students are attending school and more are graduating from high school, and the percentage who proceed into college and graduate schools has risen steadily. The American dream of universal education has come near to realization, due to favorable social and economic conditions.

Among the measures which have acted to increase school attendance are the child labor laws and the compulsory school attendance laws now in force. While laws differ from state to state, the normal rule is that a child must attend school between ages seven and sixteen, or until graduation from high school. The primary means of enforcement is through the school census, required in thirty-nine states, and by the activities of the school attendance officers. The tendency to remain longer in school was stimulated during the fifties and sixties by the exemption of college students from the military draft.

During the long period of increasing enrollments the length of school sessions has also developed until the normal school year has reached one hundred and eighty days and average daily attendance has improved through extended social services and improved health conditions, wider transportation service, and better record keeping and enforcement.

At the present time, however, counterforces are at work to limit further significant increases in school populations. These include the recent leveling of the school-age population as a result of a decreased birth rate during the fifties and sixties, and also recent rises in college tuition rates coupled with a tendency toward saturation of the market for skilled and technically trained personnel with college training.

The fact remains, however, that the proportion of young people enrolled in the schools and colleges today is greater than formerly. This has had the effect of increasing the percentage in attendance from racial minorities and lower socio-economic brackets as well as a lowering of the median in terms of intelligence and achievement—since these were the groups that formerly tended to drop out of school earlier. The curriculum of the public schools and colleges has reflected this fact, shifting from a classical, liberal arts emphasis aimed largely at middle- and upper-class clientele, toward today's more balanced offerings. The mores and folkways on school and college campuses have also shifted to match the influx of students representing all segments of our society. Among the evidences of this situation are changing standards in manners and dress, a looser moral code, and activist political attitudes. Students wish to be heard and to become actively involved in determining school policy. Where students feel frustrated in this intention, rioting, vandalism, and other forms of protest have often resulted. Students are less apt to take direction than formerly.

In addition to the altered population base in the schools, other factors are at work to influence student behavior. Relative affluence has contributed to a more permissive home life and has reduced the sense of struggle and competition which formerly motivated youth. There has been a subtle infiltration of existentialist philosophy, which holds that each person exists as an individual in a purposeless universe, requiring that he oppose a hostile environment through the exercise of his own free will. Hence, commercial and technological enterprise has been downgraded in favor of individual expression. These influences, coupled with a natural resistance to the military draft, help explain our youth's unusual preoccupation with the reform of society through an idealistic attachment to peace, environmental improvement, and population limitation. At the same time, a vast number of youth have resorted to drugs as a badge of their independence and escape. To put it bluntly, educational institutions are challenged in dealing with their charges by a range of problems which never before existed in such a degree.

Administrative response to this challenge has been mixed, ranging from permissive to authoritarian. The most useful and successful approach seems to have been to encourage full communication and exchange of ideas with the students, while carefully retaining the right of decision in all educative and operational matters. In other words, the students are properly regarded as the clients of the institution, for whose ultimate benefit all actions are taken.

Fortunately, music is a subject that lends itself to active participation of students, giving them much scope for the exercise of individual effort and judgment. Although members of a performing organization must all perform together under the director's baton, their own contribution to the ensemble is clear and unique. And there is further room for individual initiative in the solo and ensemble program. The relationship of music teachers and their students is typically quite close in all phases of private and group instruction. Students and teachers easily develop a working partnership and learn to rely upon one another. Hence, there is good communication and a minimum of misunderstanding.

In spite of this advantage, however, more attention must be paid to the assessment of the students' psychological and musical needs. This is particularly true of those students who have not become actively engaged in school music. While many of these people have developed strong interests in current popular forms and some have acquired performing abilities in this realm, they are generally repelled by or indifferent to the values of broader musical understanding. Not only is this condition damaging to them, but it exerts a drag upon the school music program and will continue as a negative influence upon music in our society.

The roots of this problem are already firmly entrenched in our culture. Students merely reflect the widespread attitude that serious music is a matter for talented professionals while popular styles belong to the unwashed amateur. The attitude is generally reinforced as a result of the usual elementary school music program. Every effort must be made there to stress the esthetic values common to all kinds of music and to break down the barriers between "youth music" and all other forms. This approach must be extended to the elective performing activities throughout the elementary and secondary schools and in the colleges. This means a broader repertoire and a greater tolerance for the expressed interests of students than is usually the case. It does not mean acceptance of sloppy performance nor a steady diet of cheap arrangements of current hits. The point is that an institution's music program should not be viewed as something exclusive, aimed at the elite. The music program must be designed to serve the needs of all the students; they must feel that it is *their* music program.

RECRUITMENT FOR MUSIC

It has just been implied that all members of a school should be regarded as participants in the music program. At the same time, some will become active participants and others will remain more passive. Deliberate measures must be taken to recruit students for beginning instrumental instruction, for membership in the choral and instrumental groups, and for enrollment in any other elective offering. In addition, assistance in making an occupational choice for music must be extended to all interested teenagers.

If it is believed that active participation in music is a good thing and should be open to all students, then the schools have a long way to go. In most cases, the opportunity for beginning instruction is severely curtailed. This is due to a succession of causes:

1. There is not sufficient preparation of the students for beginning instruction through a worthwhile general music program, including instruction on the keyboard and pre-band instruments, nor is enough familiarity established in the youngsters with the school's instrumental groups so that they may acquire the needed information and motivation to cause them to volunteer.

2. Enough instruments for beginning instruction are seldom provided. Hence, many students cannot be accepted whose parents are unable or unwilling to secure an instrument.

3. The teaching staff is too small, limiting the available instructional time and the number of volunteers that can be effectively handled.

4. The available instruction time is considered too valuable to spend upon anything except providing the future manpower for the performing organizations. Thus, seldom is beginning instruction offered in piano, or guitar, or accordion, or any such instrument not included in the band or orchestra. In fact, the orchestra is commonly overlooked. In addition, only those students who seem to have the greatest potential are accepted and these are assigned to instruments not so much upon the basis of their expressed interest as upon the needed instrumentation for the advanced groups.

5. A rigid plan for progressing to the performing groups is commonly followed, so that volunteers are accepted at only one grade level. Both the slow and the precocious are thus forced to find beginning instruction from out-of-school sources or to go without it.

6. Once the volunteers are selected and instruction has begun, the drop-out rate is often severe. Aside from dull and incompetent instruction, this result obtains from the difficulty in arranging for new trials on other instruments which might be found more suitable for individuals. Even further, there is loss because of lack of effective articulation between schools and instructors; the students are lost because insufficient measures are taken to pass them on to the next instructor. They must be recruited once again.

In view of the problems outlined above, it is no wonder that the number of instrumental musicians produced by the schools is so small. Parallel problems exist in the other phases of the school music program. The remedies are rather obvious, but administrative concern is greatly needed to ensure wider opportunity to study music and thus to create a larger body of serious music students.

Those students who are especially successful in music and achieve a strong sense of self-fulfillment in the school program are logical candidates for recruitment into the profession. Besides musical talent and achievement, a normal ingredient in the student's decision is his identification with successful musicians, often including his own music teacher. The teacher who perceives that he is being used as a model needs to proceed with care. While he wants to stimulate interest in music as a vocation, he also hopes that the students will be under no illusions. He must make clear to them the intensive preparation required, the long hours on the job, and the low extrinsic as well as the high intrinsic rewards. That is, dedication to the art of music usually results in high personal satisfaction but seldom pays off in money or status as would similar efforts in another profession.

Once a student decides to pursue music as his vocation, the choice of colleges and relative costs become important. The high cost of musical education is well known. The serious student must purchase his own musical instrument and much of the literature he will learn, and he must usually pay for the cost of individual instruction. At the same time, the student with extra talent is in great demand, since he helps make musical enterprises go. College and university music departments are somewhat trapped, since they are in competition for the especially talented ones; such individuals are needed to help produce the superior performing groups and other activities which are critical to the music education of the entire student body.

The high costs of musical instruction plus the competition for talented students has produced a system of financial aid similar to that of the college athletic program. The needy and talented, and especially those who play well those instruments that are in short supply, are subsidized by means of tuition waivers or work grants. These cover not only the undergraduates but also the fellowships and assistantships for graduate students. The costs are borne by contributors or absorbed within the fee structure and operating costs of the university.

Many universities these days, in fact, have accepted the principle that musicians should be charged no more for their professional requirements than are students pursuing the other disciplines. Hence, they do not charge special fees for private lessons, instrument and practice room rental, and the like.

Because of this difference in costs, and the greatly varying tuition charges, students are often misled by music scholarship offers; a thousand dollar scholarship from one institution may seem more valuable than the two hundred dollar offer from another—until cost comparison and distance shows that the first institution may still cost considerably more to attend. Neither does it follow that high tuition is necessarily correlated with high quality education. The young high school student preparing for a musical career must determine which college or university offers the best instruction in his particular line of endeavor and which will allow him the most scope for the exercise and improvement of his talents.

The recruiting activities of college and university music departments are designed to do just that—to acquaint the potential students with the musical opportunities at the institution and to give them a familiarity and confidence in the music faculty, plus whatever extra financial assistance is needed and available to secure the enrollment of the most highly talented.

"Shopping around" by the students gives rise to the problems in ethics among the university music departments. Excerpts from the Code

of Ethics of the National Association of Schools of Music illustrate the
scope of the matter:[1]

Article IV. Financial aid shall be awarded according to the
criteria established by the member institution granting the
award. The acceptance of financial aid by a candidate shall be
a declaration of intent to attend the institution making the
award *and he must be so informed.*

Article V. A transferring student who has not completed
a degree program can be considered eligible for financial aid
during the first term of enrollment in the new institution only
if the Music Executive of the school from which he is transferring specifically approves. Junior College transfers who have
completed a two-year program of study or whatever part of
the university parallel curriculum is available at the Junior
College attended, are exempt from this regulation.

Article VI. Institutional members of this Association
shall refuse to accept as a student, until after full investigation
of the circumstances, one who has been expelled for just cause
(disciplinary action, not academic suspension).

Article VII. Institutional members shall not make exag-
gerated or misleading statements during interviews, auditions,
nor in printed matter. All brochures, catalogs, and yearbooks
shall be an accurate statement of the curriculum, objectives,
equipment, and accommodations of the institution.

Article VIII. Advertising shall be truthful.

Article IX. Institutional members of this association
shall be at all times cognizant of the school's responsibility to
a student. Exploitation, with or without financial compensa-
tion, of a student to the detriment of his normal academic
progress shall be considered a violation of this code.

Further, when it has been determined that a student,
either graduate or undergraduate, is not acceptable as a candidate for a degree or diploma, the student shall be so informed.

ADVISEMENT AND COUNSELING

Admission to any educational institution involves establishment of
age, residency, health and physical fitness for attendance, and educational
status. In the public schools, all qualified applicants are admitted, but
most nonpublic institutions and senior colleges practice selective admission. The basis for admission depends upon the number of students
which the institution feels it can accommodate and the kind of student

---

[1] *Handbook, 1972*, Washington, D.C., pp. 18–19.

body which it wishes to serve. Many state supported universities, for example, limit admission to those who have graduated in the upper half of their high school class, or whose score on the college entrance examination ranks above the fiftieth percentile. The minimum percentile is typically adjusted upward when the number of applications becomes excessive. Certain institutions, in fact, select only those students who rank in the top tenth of their high school class.

Some schools apply other criteria for admission in the attempt to secure a more well-rounded student body. These criteria include talent in music, athletics, drama, and leadership experience in extracurricular activities. High tuition is another factor which has the effect of selective admission in terms of economic and social class, and an out-of-state tuition surcharge tends to produce geographical homogeneity. In such cases, an extensive scholarship program is often used to bring in from out of state those of exceptional talent and scholastic achievement. Large music conservatories use this system of high tuition and numerous scholarships to produce a balanced student body, with the necessary number of singers, organists, pianists, and players for each section of the orchestras and bands.

Special problems exist when admitting students transferring from other institutions, due to the variability of offerings, curricula, and standards. This is particularly the case with those students transferring from junior colleges where selective admission is not practiced; those students who are majoring in music may have the usual freshman and sophomore music courses listed on their transcripts but, due to the less rigorously selected student body, it is frequently the case that their basic work in music literature and theory has not been approached in sufficient depth, and they often lack the advantage of specialized instruction in applied music. It is right and proper, therefore, to subject these transferring students to examinations and auditions in order to ascertain their relative proficiency—and to prescribe remedial work as necessary to allow them to continue in the degree program.

The registration of students is accomplished by advisers and counselors who attempt to place them in the available courses which best suit their needs and capacities. This is an extremely complex business. By and large, the complexity increases with each higher grade level, as interests diverge and more options are provided. Even at the primary grade level, however, it is necessary for the adviser to know the pupil in order to steer him properly. The process should be approached systematically:

1. From the beginning, each student should be systematically observed and studied by teachers and counselors. Data should be recorded in personnel files.

2. Appropriate testing should be instituted, including aptitude, abilities, and achievement—and data should be recorded in personnel files.

3. Each teacher should have conferences with other teachers and specialists on students needing special attention. Data should be recorded in personnel files.

4. Each teacher should hold discussions with the students and their parents to assess progress and determine problems. Data should be recorded in personnel files.

It will be found that some students require much more attention by counselors than others do. Much of the work can be done by teachers but professional counselors are imperative. They work both with individuals and with groups. Their task is chiefly diagnostic and remedial, rather than prescriptive. The scope of problems is wide, involving personal relationships, study habits, health, program of study, occupational choice, and a sustained effort to help students become more self-reliant.

Special education is a term used to describe measures taken to care for students whose needs and capacities are found to be significantly different from the norm. These include the physically handicapped, health handicapped, emotionally disturbed, the gifted students, slow learners, and culturally disadvantaged. Many of these may be handled within the regular classes by means of special attention and individual projects, but in other cases it is found more appropriate to segregate these into groups for special instruction.

"Tracking" is a method often used to facilitate a closer match between the level of instruction and the needs and capacities of students. Under this plan, slow, medium, and fast sections of any particular subject may be established and students assigned to the appropriate section on the basis of their mental ability and achievement. This procedure, of course, is subject to criticism on the grounds of discrimination and artificial segregation. Undoubtedly, it has had the effect of killing ambition and initiative of many who have been arbitrarily confined to the slower sections. And there is much truth in the principle that fast and slow learners help one another and should be placed in the same universal situations that they face outside the school. However, tracking remains a popular technique for improving the relevance of instruction.

Promotion policy is another means by which slow and fast learners may be better accommodated. This measure is applied in the elementary schools, where some students may be required to repeat a grade and others advanced by a year or a half-year. This device is obviously dangerous to some personalities and is less popular than formerly. Most elementary schools now employ the "100% plan," whereby all are promoted in accordance with their chronological and social maturity, and the teacher is responsible to find tasks appropriate to all levels of achievement. In the secondary schools and colleges, the problem is more easily solved by advising students to enroll for lighter or heavier loads, which has the effect of adjusting their individual programs to their particular capacities and also allows stretching or compressing their period of attendance.

All music programs are fortunate in this regard, since there is an inherent opportunity for students to progress at their own rate. Each performer in a group does not have to be of the same calibre, nor must students cover the same literature in their individual lessons. There is ample opportunity for students' excess energies to be engaged in extra practice, solo performance, and creative activity.

Unfortunately, there is a tendency to blunt this effect by unnecessary limitations upon the age at which a student may elect beginning instruction, as well as the level of group in which he may participate. This is partially made necessary by difficulties in scheduling and even in transportation from building to building, but the policy does discriminate against the precocious and the "late bloomer." It should be possible for a bright youngster to begin playing an instrument a year or two before his classmates, to progress rapidly, and to make the concert band several years in advance of his peers. Similarly, it should be possible for one to begin intensive musical study in high school or even in college, and to attain membership in a performing group if his progress is sufficient.

Student advisement should be geared to allow such flexibility but, since they deal with large numbers, advisers tend to apply formulas. They have learned that exceptions to the norm are difficult to justify and often prove to be unwise, so that they are blamed for the resultant difficulties. Thus, in high schools, they have often advised superior scholars, who are also promising musicians, that music is really only an activity for them, and their schedules must be filled up with science, higher mathematics, and foreign languages in order to secure college entrance. Even those students obviously headed for a musical career are discouraged from enrolling in two music subjects during the same term, on the notion that these are not "solids" and they had better take study hall. In their turn, college advisers are preoccupied with pushing students to complete their required courses in general education as quickly as possible and also taking the necessary prerequisites in their major fields, so that their requests to join musical activities are frequently ignored. Even music advisers, entrusted with the college students majoring in music, like to follow the patterns which have been outlined for the "normal" music student—whoever he may be; very little opportunity exists for electives, substitution, and waiving of requirements to suit the individual needs of students.

Several factors can increase the possibility of individually tailored programs. One is to hold required courses to a minimum and to increase the electives. Another technique is to pre-register students into the music groups and to build the rest of their programs around those periods, so that the possibility of schedule conflicts is minimized. But most important is the attitude of the adviser; he needs to advise rather than to prescribe. Based upon his knowledge of what the student has done and desires to do, it is the adviser's job to outline the program which would seem to best fit that student. But he must also suggest alternatives. The adviser must make clear that, when the student chooses a particular course of action, certain consequences are likely to follow. When the student has finally made his choices, he must be prepared to live with the results.

When dealing with music majors, only music personnel possess the intimate knowledge of the subject and of the students that is required for adequate advisement. Thus, when general advisers are employed, much unofficial advice will be sought by the music students and given by their teachers. In colleges and universities, therefore, it is common to assign the applied music teachers as advisers of their own private students. This plan is most practical when there is a brief period for advisement followed by mass registration. But other schools have extended pre-registration to the point where advisement and registration is almost continuous; students are processed throughout each term for the ensuing term by full-time advisers and a full-time registration crew. Special music advisers for the music students thus become a necessity.

The registration machinery itself demands administrative attention to ensure a minimum of red tape. In most colleges and many high schools, students are confronted with such a maze of forms and must travel and wait in line to secure so many signatures that only the most patient types can avoid extreme exasperation. Efficiency demands that each course on the student's program, having been duly approved by the adviser, be entered immediately upon the class list; any necessary adjustments due to closed classes, etc., should be made on the spot.

RESOURCE SERVICES

Besides instruction, students require access to certain resources connected with their learning activities. For musicians, these resources include uniforms and instruments, repair service, practice facilities, reference books and scores, solo and ensemble literature, study and listening facilities, music recording and copy service.

It is obvious that one primary administrative responsibility is to see that musical instruments are made available to all who are to study an instrument and/or participate in a musical organization. Ideally, this would mean securing a complete inventory of instruments for loan or rental to the players. Usually, however, it is accomplished on the pragmatic basis of securing those instruments which the students will not provide for themselves. Since only the more serious students wish to purchase the percussion, double and lower reed, large brass, and lower stringed instruments, these are the ones which are chiefly stocked by schools, while most students can be counted on to acquire their own violins, trumpets, trombones, flutes, clarinets, and saxophones. But training programs often require that these more popular instruments also be stocked for beginning classes.

The responsibility to provide instruments as required for instruction also entails measures for their security and maintenance, through proper inventory and identification, insurance, checkout and return, storage, and repair service. Each instrument, whether school owned or privately owned, should be assigned to a locker or other secure storage facility, with ready access to the student who is playing it. Repairs must be accomplished by the school staff and/or by arrangement with commercial sources.

Another category of instruments to be provided include the non-orchestral instruments such as the classroom rhythm instruments, guitars, song bells, melody flutes, Autoharps, etc., as well as the piano and organs used in practice rooms and classrooms.

Practice rooms for individuals and small groups are a necessity in all music departments; the need may range from one or two in small high schools to hundreds in the large universities and music conservatories. Where students are living at home and may practice there, a few practice rooms will usually suffice for their use during study halls and immediately before and after school hours—but where students are living away from home, the standard formula is one practice room per each 7–10 students taking lessons. Where practice facilities are limited, a few students tend to monopolize them. This is avoided by assigning each student to a minimum number of periods per week, thus scheduling each room for occupancy throughout each day.

In addition to the materials studied in classes and rehearsals, music students need access to books, periodicals, scores, and recordings for individual study. These items are best kept under supervision in the school library or the music library and made available for use to the greatest extent possible. The rate of acquisition naturally relates to the level of schooling and student demand. Each library should contain basic, standard items, but the holdings should be much more extensive for college juniors, seniors, and graduate students in order to accommodate their investigations and research projects. Facilities for quiet study and for individual music listening are a functional part of the library service.

Students who are involved in solo and small ensemble work must have access to appropriate literature and to accompaniment service. Where large numbers are involved, a staff accompanist or other faculty member should be made responsible for securing, assigning, and assisting the accompanists. Copying service is likewise a necessity for those who do composing and arranging. Self-evaluation and learning of all student performers and composers are greatly enhanced by sound recording or videotaping and playback of their efforts. These resources should be readily available to students.

STUDENT COMMUNICATION
AND BEHAVIOR

A necessary ingredient in any effective teaching-learning situation lies in establishing healthy relationships among the students and between them and all other school personnel. The primary means to this end is that personal acquaintance should be extended as far as possible. It is well known that a group of people more easily becomes a mob when they feel anonymous, but they will act more responsibly when they feel that their individual identity is known. This is perhaps one reason why the smaller schools and colleges seem to have a greater sense of community and fewer disciplinary problems.

To achieve the closest possible relationships within large units, the administrator must first promote acquaintance and understanding by his own accessibility. He needs to appear before the student body sufficiently so that they recognize him and will not hesitate to approach him. But his reputation with students depends primarily upon the way in which his individual transactions with students have come off. Students approach him with requests for support of particular projects and for advice on their personal problems and aspirations. They seek financial assistance and propose changes and improvements in the music program. They bring him complaints about their grades, about curriculum requirements and conflicts, and about weak instruction or prejudicial treatment by their instructors. These contacts must not be sidestepped. If the administrator listens courteously, "levels" with the student, and takes positive corrective action where appropriate, then the word is passed around and the "confidence index" tends to rise.

The same sort of relationship needs to be promulgated between all the faculty members and all the students, where of course it should be easier because of their regular contact in classes. But many of these individuals develop unreasoning grudges which must finally be arbitrated by administrators. When forced to choose sides between a teacher and a student, the administrator is often confused by the conflicting charges and opinions. His most reliable guide is the past history of the individuals. Where a person has had a long record of squabbles, he is the most likely culprit. At least, that is where the search for evidence needs to begin.

Student fraternal and professional organizations are often helpful in developing social contact and good will among students and faculty, and in promoting the objectives of the unit. They are particularly good in engaging the energies of natural student leaders. Regular election or appointment of officers for the various performing organizations is also a normal means of promoting constructive leadership by students. Representatives of each group, in turn, may be selected for membership on a student council. The council should meet regularly with the chief executive of the music unit to discuss problems and issues, and may also meet on occasion with faculty committees and groups when joint problems must be met. This procedure is believed to be superior to the practice of appointing student members to faculty committees, where most points are of no immediate concern to them.

A central problem with students involves the regulation of their conduct. In former times it was acknowledged that the institution acted *in loco parentis,* to maintain the kind of conduct that the parents would enforce at home. However, much energy of young people has been recently devoted to "breaking the shackles" of adult society, culminating in the eighteen-year-old vote. With this, university students must be regarded as adults, able to determine their own actions and responsible for them. At the same time, secondary school youngsters have been moved closer to adult status.

Although educational institutions are today less concerned with dress codes and other outward manifestations of changing folkways, the need remains to regulate student conduct. Any act which may injure the educational opportunities of a student or of his associates remains within the province of the institution. All such conduct should be covered by an official code, with adequate provision for enforcement. These acts are commonly prohibited:

1. cheating or plagiarism
2. violence or threat of violence toward another person
3. arson, vandalism, theft, use of explosives
4. possession and use of firearms
5. illegal manufacture, sale, and use of harmful drugs

6. possession or consumption of alcoholic beverages on school premises
7. activity to disrupt, by force or violence, the functions of the institution
8. deliberate disobedience or resistance to the institution's officials acting in the line of duty
9. false fire alarms, bomb threats, etc.
10. giving false information, forgery, alteration of records
11. hazing
12. lewd or indecent conduct
13. continued violation of regulations concerning motor vehicles, residence halls, etc.

More common than the above violations are incipient disciplinary problems evidenced by inattention, noisy behavior, and general disregard of the rights and feelings of others. Such problems are typically faced by the individual teacher in his classes, and are best prevented by involving students in stimulating activity and efforts to build their attitude of social responsibility and *esprit de corps*. Problem students should be reasoned with and the consequences of continued anti-social behavior explained. Physical force should not be employed. Individuals who continue with deliberate violations should be subject to probation, suspension, or dismissal, and given treatment by trained professionals who may be able to uncover the roots of their problems.

PROMOTING SCHOLARSHIP
AND MUSICIANSHIP

Administrative effort needs to be coordinated with the instructors in their attempt to promote scholarly and musical achievement by the students. The means are rather obvious. Besides providing the necessary instructional facilities and resources, occasions must be created to allow students to perform as soloists and in groups. Any effective student compositions should be programmed. Competent student conductors should be featured. Excellence of scholarship should be noted. All such extra achievement should be well publicized and appropriately recognized.

Schools commonly publish a dean's list or honors list based upon scholastic records. In addition, it is often appropriate to make special awards such as the band award, choir award, or "most outstanding senior in music." These opportunities and awards are not only effective in spurring the recipients, but can have a stimulating effect upon other students in the program. It is a way of promoting higher standards and underlining the idea that talent and hard work can secure tangible recognition.

It is also highly important to promote the widest possible acquaintance with good music, other than that which the students are themselves producing or studying. For this reason, schools often sponsor attendance at local youth concerts and trips to nearby cities to attend operas and concerts. Many universities and music conservatories also require their music majors to attend a certain number of musical programs each term, taking their attendance at the door and applying the result toward a course grade. This is not for the purpose of increasing attendance, but to extend and deepen the individual's understanding of different styles of music. It also provides examples of stage deportment and audience reaction which become useful to the music student's own appearances.

EVALUATION

A major factor in dealing with students is the evaluation of their work for the purpose of marks. The problem of evaluation has already been discussed in relation to the music curriculum and the faculty; both processes relate primarily to the achievement of the students. Once again, we are concerned with evaluating student behavior, but now we must consider how marks are to be determined and reported and used.

Marks are properly based upon instructional objectives or behavioral goals to be achieved by students enrolled in a particular subject during a particular term. Although students often appeal their low marks to the administration, no one but the teacher is in a position to determine the objectives of his class, collect evidence on the student's work, and translate the result into a mark.

Percentage figures and letter grades are the most common forms of marking; other systems employ statements of relative achievement in particular aspects of a course. In either case, the difficulty arises in acquiring objective, quantitative evidence of the student's progress toward the objectives. Assignments may be made and tests may be given at the beginning, during, and at the completion of a course, but these can measure only overt manifestations of knowledge and skill. Evidence of certain types of musical understanding, attitudes, and habits must come from observing the student's recitations, deportment, and actual musical performance "under fire." Rehearsal attendance and promptness, and amounts of individual practice time, are much used criteria of attitude and habits in performing groups. All of these data can be reduced to figures useful in calculating marks.

Having attempted to quantify evidence of progress, however, the teacher is still forced in most instances to rely upon subjective judgment. He may well assign points to a certain level of accomplishment, but he is nevertheless comparing one student's work with that of his classmates or with a mythical standard of excellence. This leaves his judgment open to question by the student and other interested parties.

For another reason, it is dangerous to rely entirely upon the compilation of test scores and points in the assignment of marks. Much learning or the absence of it can be surmised by the instructor who really knows and observes his students. Hence, an instructor should always retain the prerogative of raising or lowering a mark to match his personal appraisal of a student.

As a matter of fact, the student usually wishes his mark to be based upon a numerical figure, expressing a quantitative value which he can work toward. In response to this attitude, many directors of musical organizations have developed point systems which assign points and demerits for each particular phase of behavior to be incorporated in the mark. Since membership in these organizations is usually voluntary, however, students who receive a low mark—or even a B—will tend to drop the course. In many cases, therefore, the teacher finds himself adding points to ensure high marks for all students he wishes to retain. Many institutions have gone one further step, by designating these courses for "pass-fail" grading, so that no differentiation is made between adequate and superior achievement.

Private lessons involve another segment of the music curriculum where the principle of differentiated marking is liable to break down. This is because of the close personal relationship of teacher and student and the teacher's feeling that he needs to encourage the student. Hence, we seldom see marks below a B—yet some of these students with high marks may be advised to drop their lessons due to lack of progress.

At the same time, it is often observed that students with little musical background, enrolled in introductory courses in music, must struggle to secure a passing mark. Manifestly, these people are being evaluated on standards more appropriate to music majors.

At the other end of the spectrum, at the graduate level, marks are almost confined to A and B. These people, of course, were high achievers at the undergraduate level and presented high marks for admission to graduate study. They must maintain a B average to stay in the program. But in graduate school, if materials and concepts are properly more complex and if standards are sufficiently high, one might well expect marks to slip a bit; the weaker students *should* be receiving C and D. This is part of the selective purpose of marking, which is more defensible than waiting to wash out students at a later date on the basis of their comprehensive examinations.

The whole principle of marking must be that individuals are to be evaluated on the basis of their current level and status. For example, there must be different standards for beginners and for the members of advanced performing groups; in colleges, there should be one standard for the non-musicians, and progressive standards for the undergraduate and graduate music majors. In this way, marks more truly reflect progress. They can be used as a true index of qualification to advance within the music program and for better forecasting of success in the field of music.

The administrative influence needs to be exerted to establish such a fair and equitable basis for marks, so that students in each phase and level of the music program may expect and receive marks based upon their comparative progress. This means, in essence, that the teacher should be encouraged to grade "on the curve," albeit the curve may well be skewed to account for unusual individuals and groups. The specific determination of marks for each student, however, must remain with the instructor who teaches the course and is the only one in possession of the facts necessary to make a fair evaluation. When and if a student appeals his marks to the administrator, the instructor should be consulted to see whether proper methods of evaluation have been followed. If there is doubt, a re-evaluation may be suggested, via special examination or other procedure, but any decision to change the mark must be the teacher's.

STUDENT RECORDS

One final administrative responsibility to the students lies in the keeping of adequate records of their work. A file should be maintained for each student for purposes of advisement and counseling, transfer and promotion, and job placement. It may include personal and family history, medical history, a list of courses taken and marks received, standardized test scores, the cumulative record of attendance, his music jury records and recital programs, any honors or disciplinary actions, and degrees or diplomas awarded. Such a file is indispensable in proper advisement of students and in preparing adequate recommendations for employment. Because of the highly confidential material contained in these files, they should not be open to casual inspection, but should be employed only by authorized school personnel seeking data to guide their recommendations.

QUESTIONS FOR DISCUSSION

1. What are the trends in student enrollment, their philosophy and behavior? What are the implications for administrative ap-

proach? How can the music program serve the students more adequately?

2. Review present attitudes and procedures that have a restrictive effect upon participation in school music programs. What means are available for effective and ethical recruitment of students into the music program?

3. How is selective admission practiced and what are its results? What is the proper approach to advisement and counseling of students?

4. What techniques are available to accommodate the slow and fast learners in music?

5. Describe measures that need to be taken in support of students' learning activity. What equipment and services are essential and how are these best supplied?

6. What approaches and techniques tend to improve student communications and morale? What form of student regulation will secure freedom without license? What responsibilities does the administrator have in securing adequate discipline?

7. How may the administration stimulate better musicianship and scholarship of the students?

8. What are the normal means of determining marks? What kinds of procedures in marking are especially questionable? Besides marks, what records should be kept on students?

SUGGESTED READINGS

Andrew, Dean C., and Roy DeVerl Willey, *Administration and Organization of the Guidance Program.* New York: Harper & Row, Publishers, 1958.

Arbuckle, Dugald S., *Pupil Personnel Services in the Modern School.* Boston: Allyn and Bacon, Inc., 1966.

Leonhard, Charles, and Robert W. House, *Foundations and Principles of Music Education,* 2nd ed. New York: McGraw-Hill Book Company, Inc., 1972, chap. 11.

Yeager, William A., *Administration and the Pupil.* New York: Harper & Row, Publishers, 1949.

CHAPTER SIX

fiscal management

To many a faculty member, the basic function of school administrators seems to be that of finding the money and making it available to those enterprises which most seem to require it. As we have seen, this is a gross oversimplification, since the administrative role comprehends everything it takes to organize, operate, and control a particular unit in its effort to achieve its inherent educational purposes. But it is clear that nothing will happen unless there is money to run on. And to the degree that the money is unavailable or is misspent, the unit will fall that much below in meeting its objectives. Hence, it is true that fiscal management is a primary concern of administrators.

. Except in independent music schools and conservatories, the music executive and other music faculty in administrative roles are not found at the organizational level where total operating funds must be secured and where central allocations are made. Yet they participate in decisions which may help establish the fiscal policy of the institution. Each institution is marked by somewhat different financial procedures, and new personnel soon establish working familiarity with those aspects with which they must deal. That is, one learns whom to ask for his needs, when to submit requests, what forms to complete and where to sign—but if he is to exert any creative influence upon the program he needs to understand the basic principles upon which the institution proceeds.

This chapter deals with the basic sources for funding educational institutions and their music programs, the process of budgeting, purchasing and ordering of goods and services, the essentials of accounting, and measures for reducing financial risk. Emphasis is placed upon administrative responsibilities, rather than upon technical detail, in keeping with the nature and purpose of the book.

FINANCING

As a basis for support of schools and colleges, Johns and Morphet list the following assumptions:[1]

1. Education for all should be provided through the elementary grades; for virtually all, through the high school grades; for a large proportion, through the junior or community college grades; and at least for the most competent, through the colleges and universities.

2. Throughout each state, provision should be made for an adequate program of education designed, insofar as possible, to meet the needs of every person.

3. Everyone should have an equal opportunity for the kind and quality of educational program that will best meet his needs and those of the society in which he lives.

4. Adequate educational opportunities should be provided in the public schools and at public institutions of higher learning for all who desire education in these institutions and can benefit from the program; similarly, adequate opportunities should be provided for all others in nonpublic schools and institutions of higher learning.

5. Public elementary and secondary schools should be supported by funds provided through public taxation; public institutions of higher learning should be largely, if not entirely, supported by such funds; nonpublic schools and institutions of higher learning should be supported largely on a voluntary basis.

6. Each state should provide through its constitution or laws, for adequate financial support of public schools and institutions of higher learning, wherever they may be located in the state.

7. Each citizen in the state should contribute, in accordance with his ability, to the support of public schools and public institutions of higher learning in the state.

8. The resources of the nation should be used to assist in providing educational opportunities in public schools and institutions of higher learn-

---

[1] Roe L. Johns and Edgar L. Morphet, *The Economics and Financing of Education: A Systems Approach*, 2nd ed. (Englewood Cliffs, N.J.: Prentice-Hall, Inc., 1969), pp. 6–9.

ing for the citizens of the nation regardless of the state or community in which they live.

In essence, the above assumptions say that every citizen should have an opportunity to secure the amount and kind of schooling that he requires, either in public institutions supported by local, state, and federal funds, or in nonpublic institutions supported largely by endowments, fees, tuition, and voluntary contributions. All do not agree with this premise, but it has been the basis upon which schooling has operated in this country.

It is clear that the main thrust in education has been in the public sector, largely supported by taxes, since private sources cannot and will not provide the necessary funds to educate all the citizens. Local property taxes have long been the chief support of the schools but inequality in local real estate values and in tax rates have resulted in unequal support of the schools. In turn, children in poor districts were, and are, receiving poorer quality of schooling than those in more favored areas.

Under state law, each school board has authority to levy or to call elections for levying taxes upon property up to a certain percentage of appraised value. Flat grants and matching funds have been used by states to provide the additional funds needed by the poorer districts. But continued inequities have led several states to the concept of the "foundation program." This establishes a minimum or foundation program based upon the usual elements of school programs and a standard pupil-teacher ratio, to determine standard cost per unit. Then, the total equalized property valuation for each district is multiplied by a uniform tax levy; this figure is subtracted from the cost of the foundation program to determine what shall be the state's contribution to each school district.

Federal support began in 1802, when certain public lands were granted to the schools with the admission of each new state. Each sixteenth section was granted for this purpose. The Morrill Act of 1862 granted lands for the establishment of colleges offering training in agriculture, mechanical arts, and military tactics. The Smith-Lever Act of 1914 provided for college preparation of county agents and home demonstration agents, while the Smith-Hughes Act of 1917 provided for the direct training of youth in vocational education, agriculture, trades and industrial arts, and homemaking. Certain educational experiments were undertaken during the New Deal in connection with the National Youth Administration, the Works Progress Administration, and the Civilian Conservation Corps, and the school lunch program was founded in 1935 under the Federal Surplus Commodities Corporation. The G.I. Bill of 1944, along with succeeding measures for the Korean and Vietnam veterans, contributed to the costs of those who elected to continue their schooling. These measures were followed by two others that were aimed at stimulating research—the National Science Foundation of 1950 and the Cooperative Research Program of 1954. But the big federal commitment to the support of schools came with the National Defense Education Act of 1958, in the reaction to Sputnik. This was followed in rapid succession by the Manpower Development and Training Act of 1962, the Higher Education Facilities Act and the Vocational Education Act of 1963, the Economic Opportunity Act of 1964, and three powerful measures in 1965—the Elementary and Secondary Education Act, the Higher Education Act, and the Education and Professional Development Act. By the end of the sixties, the federal government was investing at the rate of $11 billion per year in various educational enterprises. In 1971–72, approximately 7.1% of the costs of public elementary and secondary schools came from the federal government, 40.9% from the state governments, and 52% from local sources; the average per pupil expenditure during 1971–72 was $929.

Since local revenues for schools still come almost entirely from the property tax, attempts to equalize educational opportunity through state and federal contributions have not succeeded. Many poor, rural districts as well as large central city systems have considerably less money per pupil than do other more wealthy districts. For example, Beverly Hills had a pupil-teacher ratio of 17:1 and spent $1,192 per pupil in 1967, as compared with the Los Angeles pupil-teacher ratio of 27:1 and per pupil costs of $601; Evanston's pupil-teacher ratio of 18:1 and per pupil costs of $757 compared with Chicago's pupil-teacher ratio of 28:1 and costs of $571 per pupil.[2] In urban areas, the problem is compounded by the fact that (1) there are greater demands upon available revenue for "public health, safety, sanitation, transportation, public housing, and social and recreational services," and (2) "pupils who come from educationally disadvantaged backgrounds, who are impoverished, physically handicapped, nonwhite, or foreign born, all require higher than average educational services if they are to achieve at normal grade level or have their special needs met."[3]

The inequity of local support based upon a property tax has been recognized by the decision of August 30, 1971, of the California Supreme Court, which declared unconstitutional the entire financing system for that state's public schools.[4] The decision took cognizance of the fact that in 1967 expenditures per pupil ranged from $274 in one California district to $1,710 in another. Similarly, on December 23rd, 1971, a United States district court declared the Texas public school financing system to

---

[2] Joel S. Berke, "The Current Crisis in School Finance: Inadequacy and Inequity," *Phi Delta Kappan*, 53, no. 1 (Sept. 1971), 5.

[3] *Ibid.*, pp. 4–5.

[4] Reported in *Phi Delta Kappan*, 53, no. 2 (October 1971), 134.

be unconstitutional. According to the court, equal protection under the law is not being achieved because the schools in poor communities are not equal to those in wealthy areas; this is seen as a result of funding based upon local property taxes. The State of Texas was ordered to restructure its financial basis for support of the schools within two years, to achieve "fiscal neutrality." If these decisions stand, there must be a complete revision of the school support system in California and Texas, and similar moves may be expected in other states. Some have advocated that the property tax will have to be assessed, collected, and disbursed on a statewide basis, in order to correct the inherent inequities of local support. Others believe that it would be feasible to treat an entire state as a single school district, as is the case with Hawaii. In turn, a large increase in federal support is being pushed as a means to reduce inequities among the several states. A "value-added tax" has been suggested as one method of producing the needed revenue.

State-supported colleges and universities, of course, are already financed largely from taxes collected on a statewide basis and appropriated by state legislatures. Usually, their requests are prepared by administrative staffs, reviewed by their governing boards, and subjected to readjustment by a state board and/or legislative committee. Income from tuition and other receipts are estimated and cost analysis provides a basis for appropriations pegged to overall enrollment and special programs. Capital improvements, salaries, and operating costs are ordinarily funded separately.

Nonpublic schools and colleges, of course, have not been directly supported by tax monies. Yet pressures have been great to include them, and several indirect measures have been taken. Various federal and state grants have been made available to them for school lunch programs, pupil transportation, building programs, research grants, and tuition costs. There is considerable sentiment for a "voucher system," which would allot a certain amount of money for each child for his education; the parents could then send their child to any school they might choose. At the present time, however, nonpublic schools and colleges are forced to rely principally upon fee and tuition charges, endowments and gifts from foundations and private citizens, loans, sale of property, rents and receipts for services rendered. Income tax credits have been important in stimulating contributions. These same sources of revenue are also significant for public colleges and universities, which have in recent years moved toward recovering a greater share of their costs through tuition charges. Several such institutions have established the principle that tuition shall be adjusted to provide one-third of the total costs.

Local school districts ordinarily secure school buildings and other capital improvements by sale of bonds. Usually, school boards are empowered to issue bonds equalling a certain percentage of the district's assessed valuation, upon approval by the voters. However, increasingly high taxes make this process more and more difficult. In 1960, 89% of school bond issues were passed by the voters, but in 1965 only 67% succeeded, while only 48% were approved during 1970.[5] Some school boards have succeeded in bypassing unrealistic bond limits or continued negative reactions by the voters, by arranging for buildings through a School Building Authority. In effect, the Authority constructs the building and leases it to the school for a number of years under a rent-lease agreement, charges being paid from regular revenues until the costs and interest are recovered, upon which the building is deeded to the school system. College dormitories are often built under a similar plan, the debt being retired from receipts, and the buildings may then be continued in use as dormitories or converted to office or classroom use.

The major share of funds for music programs naturally comes from the sources described above. That is, musical activities occupy space paid for and maintained by sale of bonds, state appropriation, or private donations, while salaries and operating funds are allocated from those monies received into the institution's general fund from all sources. The job of the music executive, therefore, is to make his claim upon these general institutional funds in accordance with need. This is done not upon the basis of comparative enrollments, since costs vary according to the inherent instructional needs pertaining to each subject; instead, music allocations are properly calculated in terms of previous years' experience in funding the music program, plus estimates of changes anticipated due to increased or decreased costs and to additions to or subtractions from the music program.

In addition to allocations from general funds, music programs are often expected to generate additional support from ticket sales to concerts, a percentage of athletic receipts, student activity fees, lesson fees and rental charges for instruments and practice facilities, and special sales and campaigns for music scholarships and for the purchase of uniforms, instruments, trips, and the like. Funds secured in these ways are often attractive as a supplement to regular funds, and have the advantage that they may be put to unrestricted use. However, they are subject to these drawbacks:

1. They may be considered double taxation.
2. The time and effort required to produce these revenues are often educationally unrewarding.
3. Continued reliance on these sources tends to replace or reduce regular allocations.
4. The expected revenue may not materialize.

---

[5] *Phi Delta Kappan,* 53, no. 1 (Sept. 1971), 3.

As a protection to the regular allocation for instruction, such funds should always be earmarked for the support of those activities to which they specifically pertain.

BUDGETING

Budgeting is an aspect of planning which is critical to the establishment of valid educative programs. As we have just seen, the music budget is normally the means by which a portion of general revenues is claimed for the music program. It also defines the kind of program that is recommended. The budget is a financial plan which, when formally adopted, expresses the kind of music program the institution is willing to support. It also provides an instrument by which day to day control of expenditures may be exercised. A music program without a budget has to be operated haphazardly and is likely to be inefficient.

Budget preparation and administration is not a single task to be performed yearly during a certain period, but should be conceived as a continual process. To accomplish the job properly requires a major portion of administrative time and effort; such effort, however, is repaid tenfold in terms of effective, well-paced operations.

Superficially, the budget merely itemizes expected revenues and expenditures, and balances the totals. In preparing the budget document, however, several useful processes occur. Past activities must be appraised and plans for the coming year must be outlined. Costs for the planned projects must be calculated and adjusted to meet expected revenues; in doing this, continual participation in planning is required from personnel at all levels and phases of the program. This effect is further extended through the process of reviewing the budget, which acquaints higher administrative officials and the public with the needs and extent of the music program. Approval of the budget releases authority to procure the items listed therein, and to proceed with the projects to which they pertain. Finally, the fiscal officer has the information at hand to justify or to refuse individual requisitions as they arrive; he can control the rate of expenditure and make practical adjustments required by unforeseen costs or revenues.

Form of Budget

The total budget for any institution is actually a "consolidated budget" including all separate budgets for the various units. The music budget is thus one section of the consolidated budget, and may be further subdivided into instrumental activities, choral activities, etc.

And, certain operations involving musical activities may well be, and usually are, allocated within other special budgets, such as convocations and lectures, equipment, plant maintenance, etc. Certain special funds are often established, based upon receipts from student activity fees, concert or athletic receipts, and special drives, which are budgeted separately for the particular activity for which the receipts were collected. This produces decentralized budgeting. Insofar as possible, however, it is usually considered wise to prepare and administer all budgets on a centralized basis. That is, the various echelons of the organization are canvassed for their calculation of expenditures necessary to carry forward their operations for the coming year, potential receipts from every source are estimated, decisions are made on the basis of priorities to achieve the necessary balance between receipts and expenditures, and the budget document is prepared which breaks down these estimates into appropriate sub-budgets and sub-categories.

For proper administration of the music budget, the breakdown of receipts and expenditures should be made in accordance with the accounting system used by the school system or institution. For local schools, a system is suggested by the United States Office of Education, of which the main headings are given in Figure 1. A glance at Figure 1 will show that only a few of the categories are used in setting up the music budget. Other than salaries (210), allocations to music are usually made under instruction for textbooks (220), library and audio/visual materials (230), teaching supplies including music and recordings (240), and other instructional costs including faculty travel to conventions and clinics (250). Other allocations will appear under capital outlay for musical instruments (1200), plant maintenance for instrument repair (700), instrument insurance (820), and pupil transportation for music tours (500). Thus a preliminary budget estimate for a small school music program might be somewhat as illustrated in Figure 2.

Of course, other accounting systems will produce different forms of budget. One section of a fairly complex music budget is shown in Figure 3. It shows in some detail the classes of expendable supplies and services that are involved in a substantial music program.

The illustrations given are in skeleton form, however. The estimate of receipts and expenditures must be compared with last year's figures, and any large and unusual differences must be explained and justified. A small contingency fund of two or three percent is appropriately included in the budget at each level to care for unforeseen costs. Priorities are often requested or taken by implication from the order in which items are listed. All this data is employed in calculating and producing the final institutional budget.

A new approach to budgeting has been in use by the Department

Basic Revenue Accounts

(Revenue Receipts)

10. Revenue from local sources
11. taxation, appropriations
12. tuition
13. transportation fees
14. other revenue
   14-a. from permanent funds and endowments
   14-b. from temporary deposits and investments
   14-c. receipts from revolving funds
   14-d. rental of school facilities
   14-e. rental of other property
   14-f. gifts and bequests
   14-g. miscellaneous revenues
20. Revenue from intermediate sources
30. Revenue from state sources
   30-a. state
   30-b. federal money received through state
40. Revenue from federal sources

(Non-Revenue Receipts)

50. Sale of bonds
60. Loans
70. Sale of school property and insurance recovery

(Income transfer accounts)

80. Received from other school districts in state
   80-a. tuition
   80-b. transportation
   80-c. miscellaneous
90. Received from school districts in another state

Basic Expenditure Accounts

100   Administration
110   salaries
120   contracted services
130   other services

200   Instruction
210   salaries
   211   principals
   212   consultants and supervisors
   213   teachers
   214   other instructional staff
   215   secretarial and clerical
   216   other salaries for instruction
220   textbooks
230   school libraries and- audio/visual
240   teaching supplies
250   other

300   Attendance
400   Health
500   Pupil transportation services
600   Operation of plant and equipment
700   Maintenance of plant and equipment
800   Fixed charges
810   employees' retirement
820   insurance and judgments
830   rental of land and buildings
840   interest on loans
900   Food services
1000   Student body activities
1100   Community services
1110   recreation
1120   civic activities
1130   public libraries
1200   Capital outlay, sites, buildings and equipment
1300   Debt service from current funds
1310   principal on debt
1320   interest on debt
1330   sinking fund
1340   school housing authority
1400   Outgoing transferable accounts

FIGURE 1

Allocations and Receipts		*Line Item*	*Expenditures*
	220	Textbooks	
		set of songbooks for grades 5 and 6	$ 200
	230	Library and audio visual	
		music magazines	50
		music books	100
		film rental	150
	240	Teaching supplies	
		band music	500
		choral music	500
		ensemble and solo music	300
		recordings	400
	250	Other	
		convention travel	200
	500	Pupil transportation services	
		band and choir to district festival	350
music allocation	700	Equipment maintenance	
		overhaul sousaphone	300
from general		overhaul bass clarinet	75
funds $7,000		piano tuning	175
		uniform and robe cleaning	400
concert		minor instrument repairs	400
receipts 600			
	820	Insurance	
instrument		insurance on school instruments	300
deposits 380			
	1200	Capital outlay	
from athletic		· office desk	80
receipts 800		50 music racks	500
		2 double horns	1,100
		1 bassoon	700
		2 pianos @ 750	1,500
		1 tape deck and amplifier	500
$8,780			$8,780

FIGURE 2

of Defense since 1961 and is being introduced to a number of colleges and universities. It is called P.P.B.S. (Planning-Programming-Budgeting-Systems), or simply "program budgeting." Such a budget "cuts across conventional departmental lines and measures the performance of a program in terms of output. In this manner, program elements which are possible substitutes for others are given full consideration; thus program budgeting introduces a degree of competition designed to produce

Allocations and Receipts		Line Item	Expenditures
	200	**CONTRACTUAL SERVICES**	
	202	art and engraving typesetting	$ 40
	203	telephone	3,500
	205	freight charges	100
	220	maintenance office machines	500
	221	maintenance furnishings and equipment	50
	225	maintenance musical instruments	2,000
	232	rental of motor vehicles	1,000
	234	rental of costumes, cap and gowns, etc.	300
	235	rental of music and films	300
	238	rental of electrical equipment	200
	245	professional and technical services	3,400
	247	laundry	150
	251	unskilled services	250
	259	commissions and royalties	800
	260	rental of physical facilities	200
	266	postage	1,500
	273	advertising	1,200
	275	subscriptions	50
	278	entrance fees and association dues	250
	279	finance expense	10
	280	photographic service	100
	282	physical plant service	4,400
	286	transportation service	1,000
	289	stenographic service	1,200
	290	convention travel	2,500
	291	staff travel	1,700
	292	interviewee travel	300
$27,000			$27,000
	300	**COMMODITIES**	
	302	audio/visual supplies	175
	304	office supplies	220
	306	fine arts supplies (music)	2,400
	308	photographic supplies	20
	316	general stores	3,000
	317	surplus property	75
	319	printing service	3,800
	320	phonograph records and supplies	900
	330	structural and maintenance tools	150
	331	structural materials and supplies	1,000
	333	technical manuals	50
	335	theatrical supplies	1,300
	345	signs	100
	346	janitorial supplies, keys	150
	359	instructional supplies	120
	365	luncheons and entertainment	90
	367	household supplies	30
	370	wearing apparel	1,920
	372	parts, electronic, etc.	1,500
$17,000			$17,000

FIGURE 3

greater effectiveness."[6] This form of budgeting is designed for long-range planning—five to ten years—and focuses upon ways and means of achieving institutional objectives rather than upon the costs of continuing current functions. In short, it involves the reorganization of budget categories to reflect specific purposes of the various phases of the music program. Figure 4 illustrates the primary breakdown of the P.P.B.S. into programs and sub-programs. These are further subdivided into program categories, sectors, sub-sectors, and elements (i.e., individual courses, projects, etc.).

Of course, part of the idea is to establish a more convenient pattern lending itself to cost/benefit analysis via computer technology. There is no doubt that music administrators in large and complex institutions will be increasingly involved in such carefully controlled budgetary procedure.

BUDGET PREPARATION

As may be imagined, preparation of the annual budget is of central importance to the financial operation, and becomes a major coordinative task. A budget calendar is often employed to assist this process. It stipulates certain dates on which lower echelons must submit recommendations for salary raises, new positions, new programs, and preliminary estimates of operational expenditures. After this preliminary survey and upon receipt of information on revenues from major sources, the higher administration is in a position to make specific allocations to the major divisions within the institution, where in turn the different programs are revised and adjusted to meet these figures. A final deadline is instituted for assembly of all data and preparation of the document for presentation and approval by the Board.

The final institutional budget is necessarily a rather elaborate document. Being subject to close scrutiny by the Board and by the public, it must contain the answers to questions that may be asked. Besides the title page, cover letter, and table of contents, it will include a statement of philosophy and goals of the institution and a forecast of future directions. The classified breakdown of expenditures and receipts will be accompanied by supporting data. Trends will be established by comparisons with past and future budgets.

More than the mechanical assembly of requests, however, budgeting at any level demands critical thinking from each fiscal officer. He will

---

[6] Clarence Scheps and E. E. Davidson, *Accounting for Colleges and Universities* (Baton Rouge: Louisiana State University Press, 1970), p. 117.

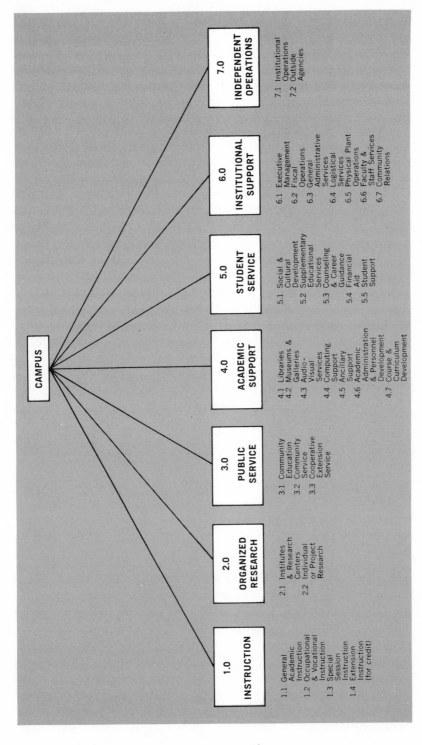

Figure 4. Organization of the Program Classification Structure. From Warren W. Gulko, Program Classification Structure (Boulder, Colo.: Western Interstate Commission for Higher Education, 1972), Figure 1.1, p. 19.

always be faced with more needs than he can fulfill. It boils down to the fact that he must stimulate creative thinking and planning within his unit and then translate these needs into priorities. This process is always based upon one's understanding of the entire scope of his operations. What is the comparative situation in each of the current music classes and activities? What items are essential to maintain these at present levels? Which phases of the program are expanding and what will these require? Where have past shortages most severely hampered the operation? What is needed to remedy this? Where are the gaps in the program that may now be filled in? What items are needed to make a good start in those directions? In short, one needs (1) to ascertain which elements in the operation should be trimmed, strengthened, or added, (2) to know what is required in order to carry out these plans, and (3) to discover how much each item will actually cost. Only then is he in a position to determine how best to distribute the available funds.

Budget decisions are always hard, but during the financial crisis facing education in the seventies they are going to be even more difficult. Music programs are likely to be affected even more than other subjects. The music executive must be prepared to build an "austerity budget" in response to "hold the line" appropriations and cutbacks. What can be abandoned with the least damage? The answer, of course, is whatever is considered optional or subsidiary in the education of the students. These items will vary with the local situation, but every effort must be made to retain the essential musical classes and activities, along with the size and quality of faculty necessary for their proper conduct. Sufficient space, good musical literature, and basic equipment must always be at hand. First to go must be trips, new uniforms, and any projects which seem to be aimed more at the entertainment of the public than at the education of the students.

Budget Administration

If the budget is to be properly effective, expenditures in each category must be kept in line with the allocations. This is done by control of the volume and rate of expenditure. Through proper accounting, a monthly classification and summary of all items ordered and received is produced, together with declining balances in each line item. Succeeding requisitions need to be compared with these balances in order to estimate how closely expenditures are matching the forecast. Expenditures can then be curtailed or increased accordingly, within the several categories, and adjusted according to new priorities. When necessary, expenditures may be temporarily "frozen" to avoid raiding and depletion of funds for certain activities at the expense of others.

Budget reappraisal, usually occurring after mid-year, is another method by which administrative control is exercised. In effect, each echelon reviews its expenditure and rebudgets its balances in the attempt to forestall any significant shortages and surpluses. Where necessary, funds are transferred and allocations are revised accordingly by higher echelons to meet the new estimates.

Great difficulties sometimes arise at this point due to rigidly conceived allocations. That is, certain allocations may be considered fixed and not transferable to meet expected shortages in other areas. This situation often stems from the fact that the original appropriations were so earmarked by legislative or board action. Many times, however, these transfers are ruled out merely to suit bureaucratic convenience and may still be arranged if the need is well documented and presented at the proper time.

Ideal budget administration not only acquires everything planned, and at the lowest cost, but results in a final zero balance of receipts and expenditures. While a deficit is damaging and often requires emergency juggling of accounts, it is equally embarrassing to finish the year with a significant cash balance, for it is evidence of poor planning and administration, and will almost certainly result in reduced allocations in future years. Thus, there is a tendency to stockpile items just at the end of the fiscal year, using unexpended funds. But it is better to run out of funds entirely just before the close of the year, having already secured or placed on order everything necessary to operate until new funds become available.

At that time, usually during May, the music executive is wise to have requisitions at hand for fairly substantial items which would be useful to the music program but which were not assigned a high enough priority for inclusion in the current or succeeding year's budget. Such items may often be acquired through unexpended contingency funds held by higher administration for emergencies which did not develop.

PROCURING GOODS AND SERVICES

Although three-fourths of expenditures in educational institutions ordinarily go to salaries, the purchasing of other goods and services remains a large item requiring careful administrative control. Purchasing is regulated by law, by the courts, and by policy of the governing boards. In general, large items must be put out on bid to avoid overpricing, and faculty and other school personnel are ordinarily prohibited from profiting by taking orders, supplying goods, or receiving rebates. A purchasing agent is usually designated in order to centralize buying operations; in small schools this is the head of the institution, in medium-sized schools buying is generally controlled by the business manager, and in large institutions there is a purchasing office.

However, the basic decisions on purchasing must remain with the fiscal officer whose account is to be charged. It is he who must determine what is needed and its specifications, indicate the quantity required, determine the time and place of delivery, and arrange for its care and storage. He must be aware of the development of new products and models, and of the need for expansion and of curricular changes and experimental programs which may dictate the acquisition of additional items to meet the educational needs of students. Too often, music personnel are not consulted in the purchase of the equipment they must employ, with the tragic result that the new rehearsal chairs may have seats that are sloping and too low for good posture, audio systems may be secured which are too small and weak for quality musical reproduction, and so on. Mass buying is not always efficient. The principle to follow is the greatest return for the dollar, consistent with the welfare of the student.

For efficient purchasing, the following procedure is standard:

1. *Product selection.* The individual discerns the need for an item which is not on hand or is found in short supply. He turns in his request through normal channels, where it is determined whether it is chargeable to a current budget allocation or must be held over for consideration with next year's requests.

2. *Requisition.* As soon as it is decided to order an item, it is necessary to determine whether previous orders can be duplicated for better standardization or whether new specifications are in order. Complete specifications are then entered on a requisition form, which is approved and forwarded to the purchasing office.

3. *Quotation.* The vendor is asked for a quotation, or bids are advertised as required.

4. *Purchase order.* A purchase order is prepared on the basis of the requisition and the quotation or lowest bid, and copies are forwarded to the vendor and to the receiving and accounting offices.

5. *Receipt of goods.* Upon receipt, the item is checked and the invoice and receiving report are signed, and an approval voucher is sent to the fiscal officer. The voucher is signed and forwarded to the disbursement office.

6. *Payment.* Payment is made on the basis of the bill and approved voucher, and payment is charged to the appropriate account.

7. *Distribution.* The item is brought to the location where it will be stored and used. Expendable supplies and commodities are entered on the stock list and permanent equipment is marked and placed on the inventory list. Users are notified of the availability of the article and any rules affecting its usage.

Services are procured on a similar basis, except that "work orders" for internal services, and "agreements for services" for external personnel, are used in place of requisitions.

Sometimes purchases of an emergency or extraordinary nature are authorized without requisition. In such case, the purchasing office assigns a "C" (control) number for specific purchases from local vendors, which number is entered upon an invoice voucher that is signed by the vendor as the items and the sales slip are picked up. The order is then processed for payment in the regular way.

Numerous special procedures are involved in processing wages and salaries, travel expenses, moving expenses, service contracts, library charges, insurance claims, medical payments, rental and lease of buildings and equipment, telephone and postal services, disposition of equipment, and the like. Each such transaction must be handled in accordance with the regulations established by the institution and outlined in its manual of business procedures.

FINANCIAL ACCOUNTING

Accounting is not something the administrator does, but something he uses. It is the process by which a complete history of all financial transactions is provided. It includes the recording, accumulating, presenting, summarizing, and interpreting of financial data, and thus provides the concise summary necessary to the exercise of fiscal control.

Three steps are involved in producing the required data:

1. Copies of all documents used to initiate and complete financial transactions are forwarded to the accounting department. These include payrolls, requisitions, purchase orders, work orders, receiving reports, invoice-vouchers, travel expense vouchers, etc., by which authority is given to procure goods and services and to make payment.

2. All items are analyzed and classified in terms of debits and credits to be entered in the appropriate accounts.

3. Information is usually computerized and entered on monthly reports for each account. Available balances are indicated, and rate of expenditure may be compared with that of the previous year. Two basic systems are employed: (1) cash accounting, which records the transaction after the bill is received and paid, and (2) accrual accounting, which enters the estimated charge as an encumbrance when the order is approved, and then enters the actual charge and credits the encumbrance when payment is finally made. Accrual accounting is greatly superior to cash accounting, since the available balance gives an up to date picture of the true balance.

	Date	Transaction Code	Transaction Number	Enc No	Beg Bal & Stu Act Fee Alloc & Receipts	Disbursements	Unexpended Balance	Outstanding Encumbrance	Available Balance
BEGINNING BALANCE					.00				
STUD ACT FEE ALLOT					6,131.20				
RECEIPTS TO BEG OF MO					.00				
ADJS TO BEG OF MO									
TOTAL BEG OF MO					6,131.20	2,042.66	4,088.54		
TRANSACTIONS THIS MO									
140 STUDENT WAGES									
P/R 08/15/1-08/28/1	09-08-1	57	785	00000		83.20			
P/R 08/29/1-09/11/1	09-22-1	57	918	00000		3.20			
203 TELEPHONE SERVICE									
SEP CHGS TELEPHONE	09-29-1	54	1041	00000		32.55			
235 RENT FILM, MUSIC									
ASSOC MU PUB	08-13-1	80		74218				40.00	
BELWIN-MILLS PUB	08-13-1	80		74217				40.00	
282 PHYS PLANT SERV									
AUD CHGS PHYS PLANT	09-09-1	54	863	00000		33.04			
306 FINE ARTS SUPPLIES									
EUGENE BAILEY CO	09-22-1	80		74341				20.00	
EUGENE BAILEY CO.	08-25-1	80		00012				10.50	
TOTAL TRANSACTION THIS MO						151.99		110.50	
ADJS TO STUD ACT FEE					.00				
STUD ACT FEE ALLOT-MENT					6,131.20				
RECEIPTS TO DATE					.00				
TOTAL TO DATE					6,131.20	2,194.65	3,936.55	110.50	3,826.05

FIGURE 5

The monthly statement on page 128 (Figure 5) illustrates the method of accrual accounting. In this instance, $2,042.66 has been spent through August of the $6,131.20 originally allocated, leaving a balance of $4,088.54. Additional expenditures of $151.99 during the month of September have brought the unexpended balance to $3,936.55; however, the further amount of $110.50 has also been encumbered, leaving an available balance of $3,826.05 for October 1 through June 30.

Such a statement is indispensable for an accurate check of items received and costs incurred, and serves as a guide in adjusting expenditures for succeeding months. It also provides part of the data needed in auditing the account and helps to serve as a basis for budget estimates for the ensuing year.

Separate accounts are established by the accounting office for each separate fund which is entrusted to a specific fiscal officer, as well as a general control account which incorporates all the individual accounts within the general fund. Other accounts are established for special activity funds, revolving funds, trust and agency funds, building funds, etc.

PROTECTING FUNDS, PROPERTY, AND PERSONS

Administrative fiscal responsibility does not end with funding, budgeting, purchasing, and accounting, but includes measures to minimize risk to monies, physical properties, and personnel. Regular procedures must be established to deal with these matters.

The important thing with cash receipts from ticket sales, fees and deposits, and the like, is to keep adequate records of such receipts and to transfer them immediately to the official who is appointed to receive and deposit the funds. To leave cash pertaining to school functions in the hands of individuals risks theft, loss, and unaccountable expenditure.

Excess funds in significant amount which are not subject to immediate expenditure should be invested on a short-term or long-term basis in order to attain maximum value.

Surety bonds are advisable for any personnel who must deal directly with school funds of any magnitude.

Regular audit is another method of protecting against misuse of funds. Auditing is simply a careful review by disinterested personnel of all documents giving evidence of financial transactions. The objectives of an audit are:

1. to determine that all financial transactions have been recorded and entered in the proper accounts.

2. to determine that the recording is verified by another.
3. to verify prices, quantities, and receipt of goods and services.
4. to determine that balances are properly computed.
5. to provide safeguards against theft and against removal of items without proper authority and without necessary measures to insure return.
6. to provide clerical control over journals, registers, summaries, ledgers, and reports.

An internal audit is accomplished by appointed school personnel and may be employed for individual accounts and periodic checks. However, an external audit by an independent firm is necessary to establish absolute integrity of fiscal management.

Various types of insurance are useful in protecting capital investments such as buildings, heavy equipment, and musical instruments. State insurance, where available, reduces costs because no profit is involved. Indeed, many state universities and extremely large school systems are self insured by virtue of the great amount and dispersion of the property; it is figured that replacement of even major losses can be borne as easily as could the insurance premium to cover all items. However, liability insurance is another thing; to protect against major claims for accidental injury and death, liability insurance covering all employees, students, and patrons on school property or school sponsored activities is a necessity.

Group life insurance, medical and hospitalization plans, and retirement plans are other forms of insurance which schools usually provide or contribute to for their employees. These "fringe benefits" have become major factors in employee protection and are ordinarily negotiated between the carriers and the administration and committees representing the local teachers' association or union.

It may be seen that good fiscal management is designed to assure the necessary flow of funds to the right place at the right time in order to achieve the goals of the institution. All school personnel are involved in the process, under administrative control. There is no place for favoritism nor arbitrary, capricious decisions. Decisions must be based upon hard reality, but need to expedite rather than impede operations. The administrator should realize that the funds under his control do not belong to him but belong to the institution; he is accountable to its members as well as to those who provided the funds. No special interest group should be given undue influence in determining allocations nor should the administrator become enmeshed in "pet projects" which would drain resources from the main elements of the educational program. He must always be able to justify the allocations he has made.

Just as a bank is unafraid to loan money to those who seem to need it least, good fiscal management produces confidence where funds are generated and makes it easier to justify and secure additional funds. Operations will more nearly follow plans and emergencies will seldom arise. The potential of the institution will be more nearly realized.

QUESTIONS FOR DISCUSSION

1. Is it true that every citizen deserves an education? How far does such responsibility extend? Who should pay for this education?
2. To what extent have the federal government and state governments supported the schools and colleges, and how does this compare with local support? What has been the traditional form of taxation for the local school district?
3. Why has the current basis for school support been under heavy attack as discriminatory? What changes seem to be in prospect for school support? What will be the likely result of these trends?
4. What is the financial situation of non-public schools and colleges? What are their main sources of revenue?
5. What are the sources of funds for musical instruction and how are these claimed or generated?
6. How is the music budget developed? How does it relate to the institutional budget? How is it tied to the institutional accounting system?
7. What differences in budget thinking and format are involved in program budgeting?
8. What is the basis of decision to include or not include items within a budget? What techniques are useful in budget administration?
9. Trace normal purchasing procedure.
10. What is the role of accounting in fiscal managment? What information does the monthly statement of accounts provide?
11. What measures are useful in protecting against loss and misuse of funds and property?

SUGGESTED READINGS

Casey, Leo M., *School Business Administration*. New York: Center for Applied Research in Education, Inc., 1964.

Farmer, James, *Why Planning, Programming Budget Systems for Higher Education*. Boulder, Colorado: Western Interstate Commission for Higher Education, 1970.

Jervis, Oscar T., Harold W. Gentry, and Lester D. Stephens, *Public School Business Administration and Finance*. West Nyack, N.Y.: Parker Publishing Co., Inc., 1967.

Johns, Roe L., and Edgar L. Morphet, *The Economics of Financing Education*, 2nd ed. Englewood Cliffs, N.J.: Prentice-Hall, Inc., 1969.

Mort, Paul R., Walter C. Reusser, and John W. Polley, *Public School Finance*, 3rd ed. New York: McGraw-Hill Book Company, Inc., 1960.

Osview, Leon, and William B. Castetter, *Budgeting for Better Schools*. Englewood Cliffs, N.J.: Prentice-Hall, Inc., 1960.

Roe, William H., *School Business Management*. New York: McGraw-Hill Book Company, Inc., 1961.

Tidwell, Sam B., *Public School Fund Accounting: Principles and Procedures*. New York: Harper & Row, Publishers, 1959.

University of the State of New York, *Insurance*. Albany, N.Y.: State Department of Education, 1963.

CHAPTER
SEVEN

providing
music facilities

Many subjects may be taught with a minimum of space and equipment, but music is not one of them. A vast array of musical instruments and audio equipment must be stocked and kept available for use. Besides regular classrooms and offices, special rehearsal rooms are required for the large performing groups, and large halls must be available for their performance. In addition, teaching studios are needed for individual instruction and small rooms for individual practice. Specially equipped rooms for study and listening are desirable. Very difficult problems arise in storing, securing, and servicing all these facilities.

Not only does music require large quantities of space and equipment, but the specifications are unique. The type of sound reflection within rooms is critical to educational results; and equally important is the reduction of sound transmission between rooms to levels that do not interfere with instruction. Adequate lighting is extremely important to the study and production of music, while proper ventilation and temperature control are absolutely imperative to the welfare of the individuals and the equipment involved in musical activities.

The heavy responsibility of the music administrator in meeting all of these problems is obvious. Unfortunately, they are not often fully appreciated by his faculty colleagues and fellow administrators, nor even by many architects who work on school buildings. In his effort to achieve the necessary facilities for music instruction, the music administrator must often appear to be unusually demanding, impractical, and fussy. Yet the job must be done by one means or another.

This book is especially addressed to music educators who work in all kinds of situations, ranging from very small to very large music departments. They will be faced at various times with the need to expand or to contract their facilities, to move to different quarters, or to participate in planning new facilities. Our discussion, therefore, is aimed at broad comprehension of problems and solutions, rather than at formulas for constructing an ideal plant. We will outline principal considerations involved in the various types of music rooms, recommend procedures to be followed in planning new facilities, and discuss the kinds of equipment that need to be provided. We will also deal with the storage and maintenance of that equipment and the proper service and control of music facilities.

MUSIC ROOMS

Space for musical instruction may be especially built for that purpose, or "inherited." In the case of auditoriums and classrooms, the space may be jointly used with other school activities. Of special concern are the design of the various rooms for sound and the proper accommodation of personnel, their relative locations, and the arrangements to avoid intrusive sound transmission between rooms.

Room Location and Acoustics

In general, music facilities should be located at a distance from other academic facilities, since the musicians can bear the sound problem better than can their academic colleagues. Where a separate building is not possible, a separate wing is advisable. But also within the area for music, dispersal is a useful thing, for this reduces the difficulty with sound transmission. That is, single-floor construction is preferable because less acoustical problems are involved with the floors and ceilings. Sprawling, multi-corridor construction further reduces the number of interior walls which have to be specially constructed to reduce sound transmission. This type of facility occupies more land and goes counter to the usual rule that large cubicle buildings are less costly per square foot, but it has been found that music buildings are an exception to this rule.

Even within the building, it is useful to have corridors, offices, and storage areas located between the various teaching and performing locations, in order to help attenuate sound.

On the other hand, certain rooms need to be in close proximity because of common usage and convenience in moving equipment and personnel. Band, orchestra, and choral rehearsal rooms are best located just across the hall from the auditorium stage for ease in setting up performances and to allow common use of equipment. Certain storage facilities and teaching studios need to be nearby for better supervision and security.

Proper insulation of music rooms becomes crucial where sufficient dispersal cannot be arranged. Many believe this is done by placing sound absorptive materials on the walls, whereas this chiefly affects the internal acoustics of the room. Soft, porous materials tend to absorb sound, while hard, smooth surfaces reflect it. Sound passes readily through light, thin materials and is held back by density and thickness. But partitions, beams, and openings always carry sound between adjacent areas. To secure needed insulation, therefore, the job is to provide heavy barriers, to disconnect the sound transmitters, and to plug the openings.

Where buildings are originally constructed for music, therefore, the walls need to be of thick, dense materials and certain walls may need to be of double slab construction, with insulating material or air space between the slabs. Beams between rooms need to be jointed, to break sound transmission. Between two floors, double ceilings may also be constructed. Where sound isolation is especially critical, entire rooms are constructed within rooms, by "floating" construction.

Special attention is also required with heating and ventilating ducts, which simply transport sound from room to room unless they are well baffled and lined with sound absorptive materials. Doors should be of hollow core construction, soundstripped, and with latching devices to ensure a firm seal. Double pane windows seated in rubber are also helpful in reducing sound transmission.

Unfortunately, all these measures for sound isolation add to costs and it is sometimes rather difficult to convince school administrators and architects of their necessity. Hiring a good acoustical consultant who can ensure proper technical detail is good economy in planning construction of new music facilities.

Where general space is taken over by music departments, as is often the case, acoustical problems are likely to be severe, but certain measures can still be taken. Careful appraisal will show where new doors should be installed, where ventilating ducts need to be insulated, and where new interior walls may need to be constructed. Sometimes, judicious addition of absorptive wall and ceiling tile will be helpful.

Interior room acoustics is a product of the room volume and distances, and the reflective and absorptive values of the various room surfaces. The sound waves travel to the listener by various routes and reach him at different times and with different frequency and intensity. At least five important factors must be controlled:

1. *Intimacy* is determined by the "initial time-delay gap," which is the measure of difference between the time when the direct sound reaches the listener and the arrival of the first reflected sound. Figure 1 illus-

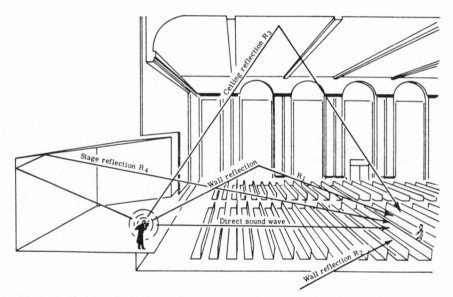

Figure 1. Showing the paths of direct sound and several reflected sound waves in a concert hall. Reflections also occur from balcony faces, rear walls, niches, and any other reflecting surfaces. From Leo J. Beranek, Music, Acoustics, and Architecture *(New York: John Wiley and Sons, Inc., 1962).*

trates this principle. A large, open hall will naturally produce a large initial time-delay gap and a hollow effect—unless side balconies or suspended sound reflecting panels are employed to produce quicker reflection.

2. *Liveness* is a product of "reverberation time," or persistence of the sound due to reflection. The proper amount of reverberation enhances the tone and varies with the size of the hall and the kind of music being produced. For example, a pipe organ played in a large hall may sound best with a two and one-half second reverberation time, whereas a half

second reverberation time will be about right for a piano played in a small practice room. Figure 2 illustrates the range of reverberation time

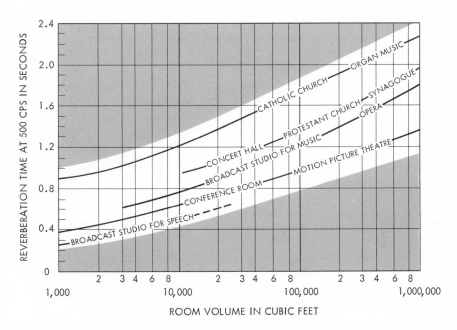

Figure 2. Optimum reverberation time for rooms of various sizes. From Richard Bolt, "Acoustics," in Music Rooms, Buildings, and Equipment, *ed., Charles L. Gary (Washington, D.C.: Music Educators National Conference, 1966), p. 76.*

suitable to different sizes of rooms. Sound waves are reflected back and forth around a room, subject to natural decay, unless they are more quickly absorbed. Thus, the actual reverberation time is a product of the cubic volume of the room and the amount and distribution of absorptive values within the room, including the people. Normally, one needs to extend the reverberation of large halls by use of smooth plaster and thick wood, while reverberation usually needs to be reduced in small music rooms through liberal use of acoustical materials. But these arrangements need to be accomplished by applying the formula, rather than by guesswork.

3. *Warmth* of tone results from proper reverberation of the bass tones. These lower frequencies are prone to penetrate thin partitions and to become lost.

4. *Strength of direct sound* is a critical factor in producing a natural effect in large halls. It is promoted by good shell design to pick up and project sound from the performers to the audience, and by stage risers and sloped audience seating to maintain unobstructed lines of sound travel between the performer and each listener.

5. *Good sound diffusion* is produced in rooms with irregular surfaces of different materials, so that sounds are randomly reflected and thoroughly mixed. The result is a natural sound, without prominent echoes or other distortions.

AUDITORIUMS

Music activities are greatly dependent upon access to a hall or halls where public performances will be presented. A medium-sized concert hall, seating 500 to 1,000 and designed for listening, is the ideal setting for musical activities in most educational institutions. Such a hall has a stage which will accommodate a full-sized orchestra or band and which is designed as an acoustical shell for best sound projection. In such case, another theatre type hall is necessary for the production of plays and other staged works, such as musicals and opera, featuring a large stage house built to fly scenery and containing full stage rigging and lighting facilities, sufficient wing space, dressing rooms, and working space necessary for building and storing scenery and other stage properties; such a hall also requires an orchestra pit of comfortable dimensions, preferably with a floor which serves as a hydraulic lift capable of being raised to stage level in order to allow extension of the stage and the transport of heavy equipment to and from below-stage. Either kind of hall requires theatre type seating for the audience, moderately raked (inclined) to ensure unobstructed view and sound. Construction should feature plaster and thick wood paneling to enhance reverberation, and balconies may be used to increase seating capacity without increasing the listeners' distance from the stage.

Unfortunately, due to the high cost of separate halls for concert and for staged works, music departments must usually be content with a single multi-purpose hall. Of necessity, this is a theatre with a movable acoustical shell on stage, or an acoustical ceiling which can be lowered and extended above the concert groups to reduce dissipation of sound within the stage house and to reflect it toward the audience.

In too many situations, no hall is available except a school gymnasium, ballroom, or cafeteria; some of these possess a stage enclosure in one wall, and the audience is seated on folding chairs facing the stage. Another arrangement is simply to place the performers in the center of the gymnasium floor, facing the bleachers. Acoustical problems are usually severe in such structures. Risers for the performers and proper acoustical treatment of the walls and ceiling can be of some help.

REHEARSAL ROOMS

Wherever possible, special rooms should be provided for the rehearsal of the large performing organizations. Such rooms should be designed to seat all the players or singers in regular concert formation. No supporting columns should be used. Some prefer a flat floor for greater flexibility, but others favor risers for more direct sight lines and better sound. If risers are used, they should be three feet wide for singers and four and a half feet wide to accommodate instrumentalists. A diameter of fifteen feet is suggested for the interior semicircle where the conductor and the first row of performers will be situated.

Rehearsal rooms should be of generous proportions. For acoustical reasons, the ceiling should be at least seventeen feet high. At least eighteen square feet are needed per performer, which means that a group of ninety students needs a room sized 32' × 50'. This allows sufficient space for their seating, for pianos and percussion instruments, and for the space at the front and sides of the room needed to allow passage and access to adjacent storage facilities. Opening into the rehearsal room will be related facilities, such as instrument repair room, percussion storage, instrument locker room or corridor, practice rooms, uniform and robe storage, music library, and directors' offices.

A room of the size described (32' × 50' × 17') should have a reverberation time of about one second, which requires moderate use of absorptive materials on walls and ceilings. Good lighting, ventilation and constant temperature control are critical to the rehearsal area for obvious reasons.

In some instances, instead of separate rehearsal rooms, the auditorium stage is regularly employed for the rehearsals of large musical groups. Equipment is kept offstage for setting up prior to rehearsal time. Besides saving the cost of extra space, this also avoids the problems of moving to a new hall for dress rehearsals and performances, and the consequent need to meet the different acoustical situation. Countering these advantages are the extra problems in security and the conflicts which are sure to arise in scheduling the facility.

Many small schools do not offer separate rehearsal facilities, but instead provide a single all-purpose room for musical activities. Of course, such a room must have the space and acoustical design required for the largest instrumental organization, plus the chalkboards, audio equipment, piano, and other facilities necessary for quick conversion to use for choral rehearsal, general music classes, individual and small group instruction.

PRACTICE ROOMS

Even very small secondary school music programs deserve two or three small practice locations, where students can practice individually during free periods and after school. Since university music students will average 1½ to 2 hours per day in individual practice, one practice room is needed for each 7–10 music students. A good usable size is fifty square feet, but there must be a few larger ones for small ensembles, two pianos, and organ. These rooms are usually situated side by side along a corridor or grouped in suites of three or four rooms placed between larger teaching studios and classrooms. In these circumstances, intrusive transmission of sound between rooms is guaranteed unless strong measures are taken for its reduction. These measures include floating construction, specially treated heating and ventilating ducts, and tightly sealed doors. Within each room, reverberation time must be very short, requiring liberal employment of sound absorptive materials.

MUSIC CLASSROOMS AND LABORATORIES

Where music is taught in general classrooms in conjunction with other subjects, suitability for music is largely a matter of seeing that the proper equipment and storage facilities are available. But special purpose music classrooms for music theory, music literature and music education, class piano, and other instruments to be taught in groups, often need to be designed to fit the activity. Theory classrooms, for example, need lots of chalkboards with painted music staves. Classrooms for music literature, conducting, and music methods have special need of fine built-in audio visual equipment. Laboratories for music listening, for electronic class piano instruction, and for electronic music composition all require masses of special equipment, permanently installed, and all of these music classrooms and laboratories demand special treatment to reduce the level of sound from adjoining rooms and hallways if instruction and study are to be suitably managed.

MUSIC OFFICES AND STUDIOS

Non-teaching offices must be supplied as needed for all music faculty who are not assigned to teach individual lessons. These can be relatively small and generally require nothing beyond the usual office furnishings and equipment. However, when applied music teaching is to occur in these locations, they become studios for individual and small group teaching as well as offices for conducting business. As such, they need to be large enough not only for office equipment but also to accommodate groups of three or four performers, along with pianos and extra storage facilities for instruments and music. These studios also need to be properly designed for good internal acoustics and for sufficient sound isolation to allow effective teaching. Tight quarters and/or a noisy environment are very poor economy in music studios, where so much of the music program is carried on.

SPECIAL FACILITIES

Depending upon the size and extent of the music program, certain special facilities may be required. These may include shops for handling instrument repair, piano repair, reed making, and audio/visual equipment, as well as reception area, faculty conference room, and student lounge. Obviously, each of these types of rooms will need to be tailored to fit its particular requirements.

UTILIZING AND SECURING SPACE

At various points in time, music units will find themselves in various situations as regards housing. If adequate planning and construction have preceded growth, then a unit will be properly housed; spaces will be assigned on a logical basis consistent with original plans and operations will proceed without major problems due to any lack of space. But this situation is likely to be only temporary. Casual observation will confirm the fact that most music units have outgrown their original quarters and many, indeed, have never succeeded in acquiring title to enough space to properly house their operation. In such case, the administrator has the problem of allocating the available spaces very carefully for maximum efficiency, securing repairs and renovation where feasible, and competing successfully for new and adequate quarters or the assignment and conversion of existing facilities to the music program.

Proper utilization of space means that all musical activities will be fitted into the most logical areas, each of sufficient size and physical properties for best accomplishing the work to be done there. In general, this means that the larger rooms will be reserved for the larger organization rehearsals and for large classes, small rooms will become practice rooms and individual offices, while medium-sized rooms will be employed as teaching studios and seminar rooms. Administrative offices will naturally be located near the main traffic arteries, while music libraries and instrument lockers will be placed near the rehearsal rooms. Since these rooms were often not originally designed with musical instruction in mind, however, it is sometimes necessary to modify general principles. Noisy activities absolutely require reasonable isolation if other activities are to proceed. The transmission of sound may be so great that large rooms situated next to rehearsal areas simply cannot be used for classes, or for teaching studios, but can only be employed for storage. Locations may dictate that two rooms be combined into one large one by removing an interior wall, while another room may be subdivided to secure several smaller locations.

With small units of two and three music teachers, space assignment is difficult enough, but in large and growing departments it often becomes acute. This is because alternative solutions are usually available, and one is dealing with individual prior rights of seniority and territoriality. Thus it is that the senior professor usually inherits the most desirable studio, while the most vigorous and successful performing group gradually acquires the most convenient rehearsal and storage areas. This principle of "survival of the fittest" may be followed unless and until it produces unsuitable conditions for operations which could have been avoided by more logical assignments. Thus, the teachers of the larger and louder instruments should be assigned to the larger studios, simply on the basis of need. The administrator must have a general plan for space occupancy which is consistent with the needs of the various activities and adjustable to changes in the program and in personnel.

As an outgrowth of his planning of space assignments, the administrator should always have a current assessment of the overall need for space based upon the present music program and a reasonable growth forecast. This assessment is properly based upon the following data:

1. Current institutional enrollment and official forecasts of enrollments five, ten, and fifteen years hence.
2. Current and past music enrollment and a reasonable projection of growth.
3. Offerings necessary and desirable to build a complete and well rounded music program for the expected enrollment.
4. Changes in the number of faculty based upon equitable faculty loads necessary to cover the above projections.
5. A summary of current space allocations and description of additional space needs to accommodate projected increases in students, faculty, and offerings.

The crucial step in acquiring facilities, of course, is in convincing those who hold the power of decision that the music program actually requires and deserves that space be added, converted, or newly constructed. The specific personnel to be convinced are difficult to identify, usually consisting of the institution's executive head and his principal staff officers, the governing board, and eventually the public. Since school construction is usually far behind need and is nearly always partially obsolescent, one may be sure that continuing pressures are exerted by other disciplines to secure additional facilities. Thus, the needs of the music program must be presented with such force that their comparative urgency is clear. The object must be to secure definition of a

but major rehearsal rooms often contain a large array of equipment. The basic item, of course, is an adequate number of chairs, easily folded or stacked but sufficiently solid and comfortable for long rehearsal. Ordinarily, one looks for chairs with seats that are level, moderately padded, and high enough from the floor for the age level to be using them (18″ for adults and high schoolers). Solid, easily adjustable music racks are also a basic requirement of instrumental rehearsal rooms—two for every three members of the largest group. Folding risers or platforms of assorted heights are necessary for staging performances and are also useful in rehearsal where fixed risers are not already installed. Narrow risers for standing choral groups are usually necessary in addition to the wider risers for seated groups. Other items commonly acquired for rehearsal rooms include chalkboard and bulletin board, electric tuner, conductor's podium and chair-stand, recording and playback equipment, music sorting rack and folio cabinet, percussion cabinet, tuba chair-stands, and stools for percussion and string bass players.

Highly sophisticated equipment is required in rooms designed for musical recording and film projection, mass listening, multiple listening with headsets, electronic piano classes, electronic composition, instrument repair, and the like. Likewise, auditorium staging and lighting equipment requires special design. Advice should be sought from experts acquainted with the latest devices and models and who understand the problems of installation.

Instruments for use in band and orchestra and in the elementary classrooms always constitute a major portion of the music department inventory. We have already pointed out that responsibility to provide these instruments rests squarely on the school insofar as the students cannot or do not provide their own. However, it is important not to overstock instruments. The administrative ideal is to see an instrument in the hands of each volunteer—one that is in tune and in good mechanical condition—and none left in storage. Any lack of instruments is educationally damaging while the storage and upkeep of surplus instruments is quite wasteful.

For obvious reasons, the selection of instruments must be based upon serviceability. Simply, which instrument will play easiest, sound best, and stay in condition longest? The original price is only a minor factor. Indeed, the best buy is usually one of the more expensive models, if adequate measures are taken to protect the investment.

Band uniforms and choir robes offer similar problems. They must be chosen to meet the specific needs of the organization, and to secure the utmost serviceability in terms of style, fit, comfort, and long wear. The best appearance over the longest period of years usually far outweighs any difference in original cost.

We have briefly reviewed basic equipment for music programs, but there is no end to the variety of articles that may be usefully employed in some phase of musical activity. The initial step of identifying the needed items often falls to the teacher who wishes to employ them, rather than to the administrator. This is as it should be. But it is easy simply to approve requests as they come in, until the money runs out; that approach penalizes those parts of the music program which are staffed by less aggressive personnel. The administrative job is to survey needs and to see that each phase of the operation has access to the most essential equipment. Then, it is possible to determine where any available remaining equipment funds may best be put to use. The administrator must continually be on his guard against extravagant "toys" that merely look functional, and equally on guard against "bargains" that will quickly prove unserviceable. He must make sure that each item of equipment is justified in terms of planned functions, and that each particular item is of the best type and design to do the job.

USE AND MAINTENANCE OF FACILITIES

It should be apparent that the hard won space and equipment for music instruction demand great care and attention in order to secure total value. Space and equipment should be employed as fully as possible, but always under adequate supervision. The administrator's first concern is security. This is achieved by the following preventive measures:

1. Properly securing all external openings to buildings, establishing practical open building hours, and assigning watchmen as necessary during closed hours.
2. Having all musical instruments and other equipment individually assigned and stored in lockers, cabinets, closets, or other controllable areas.
3. Giving access to rooms and equipment only to responsible personnel who must use the facility—and seeing that items removed for use elsewhere are immediately returned and secured.
4. Seeing that all storage areas are locked when the equipment is returned to them, and especially when the owners or regular users are not present.
5. Keeping thorough inventory of equipment and careful records of all keys and equipment on loan.
6. Acquiring insurance against fire, theft, and vandalism of buildings and equipment as authorized by the institution.

Proper storage arrangements are, of course, a key factor in the management of facilities. All equipment should be stored as near as possible to the point of normal use, yet with access to users without interference with regular operations. This means that instrument lockers need to be in the corridors just outside rehearsal and practice areas; office machines need to be in rooms adjoining the main office, ready for use; circulating tape recorders and record players need to be controlled from the music office or from the audio/visual center.

Certain personnel play a key role in the management of buildings and equipment. These include the night watchmen and the building custodians who provide janitorial service; these individuals not only clean and straighten and perform minor services, but are also important to security. Secretaries must assume heavy responsibilities for equipment in their offices and in keeping records of loaned keys and equipment. The band and/or orchestra director is often responsible for record keeping and checkout of musical instruments; in other institutions, this is the function of an instrument repair technician who serves also as equipment manager. Other classes of equipment are often entrusted to audio/visual technicians and piano technicians.

But of course the music faculty can not escape the joint responsibility to keep their own rooms and equipment secure and to keep their eyes and ears open. Lack of concern on the part of teachers about the state of the buildings and equipment will soon cause a relaxation of concern by students and custodians, so that rooms will become dirty and littered, equipment will be left unsecured and unattended, and general lacks of accountability will be accepted as the norm. To counter this tendency, it is an administrative responsibility to establish systematic procedures, assign duties, and make sure that regulations are enforced.

A special problem occurs when musical activities are temporarily moved to a different location for dress rehearsals, concerts, tours, parades, or athletic events. Danger to equipment is greater under these circumstances since the usual controls are absent. Obviously, special organization must be invoked. The move must be carefully scheduled, so that each item is listed and specific times indicated for the move and return. Supervision of such moves is necessary and arrangements are needed for the safe storage or supervision of the equipment at the temporary location. Quite detailed plans are usually necessary for touring groups, so that individual students or crews are assigned to unload, set up, and repack the different articles of equipment.

The serviceability of buildings and equipment is limited by the availability of maintenance and repair services. Without adequate maintenance, operations will soon grind to a halt. Light bulbs will burn out, fuses will blow, machines will become jammed, pianos will go out of tune, and clarinet pads will drop out. A significant portion of an administrator's time is often spent in meeting such problems so as to allow instruction to proceed.

In maintaining equipment, prevention is better than cure. Thus, a piano tuner is hired or contracted to inspect and tune and repair the pianos at specified periods. Similarly, a regular instrument repair service should be arranged through a nearby music store or with a qualified individual; part of that service will be to schedule instruments for factory overhaul as required. Unless a qualified electronic technician is available through the school, prior arrangements must be made for servicing audio/visual equipment through the local outlet or manufacturer. Service contracts for business machines should be secured. Recommendations for repair and refurbishing of all music facilities should be made whenever inspection reveals the need.

The provision of space and equipment is critical to the music program. Naturally, the complexity of the job depends upon the size and extent of the music program. The more plant and equipment that are required, the more massive are the problems of procurement, installation, security, maintenance, and replacement. The whole idea is to achieve simple efficiency, made possible by wise planning in terms of the objectives of the music program, the effective presentation of needs, and the husbanding of resources.

QUESTIONS FOR DISCUSSION

1. Why is the attenuation of sound of such importance within structures where music is to be taught? What factors in building shape and room placement are important in producing attenuation?

2. Between rooms, what measures help to reduce sound transmission? What can be done to improve existing rooms?

3. What measures are helpful in securing good sound projection of performers in a hall? What factors are important in producing the proper kind and amount of reverberation? Do larger rooms or smaller rooms generally require more absorptive treatment?

4. Describe a well-designed and equipped hall for musical events. What modifications are common?

5. Draw or describe an adequate rehearsal room for large instrumental and/or choral groups. What equipment and other facilities should be at hand?

6. What factors are important in the design and construction of music studios, offices, classrooms, practice rooms, and related facilities?

7. On what basis is space assigned to music activities and personnel? What data are helpful in claiming additional space? What are the normal steps in planning and preparing new housing for the music program?

8. What are the major classes of equipment that need to be provided for music instruction? How does one judge which items are to be acquired now, and how are the specifications determined?

9. What are the standard measures to be taken for the security of buildings and equipment? To whom is responsibility delegated for the operational control and maintenance of music facilities?

SUGGESTED READINGS

Beranek, Leo L., *Music, Acoustics, and Architecture.* New York: John Wiley & Sons, Inc., 1962.

Century Theatre Lighting. New York: Century Lighting, Inc. 1960.

Doelle, Leslie L., *Acoustics in Architectural Design.* Ottawa, Ontario: Division of Building Research, National Research Council, 1965.

Faris, Gene, *Guidelines for Audiovisual Personnel and Equipment, 1965.* Washington, D.C.: National Education Association, Department of Audiovisual Instruction, 1965.

Gary, Charles L., ed., *Music Buildings, Rooms, and Equipment.* Washington, D.C.: Music Educators National Conference, 1966.

House, Robert W., *Instrumental Music for Today's Schools.* Englewood Cliffs, N.J.: Prentice-Hall, Inc., 1965, chap. 7.

Tiede, Clayton H., *The Practical Band Instrument Repair Manual.* Dubuque, Iowa: William C. Brown Co., 1962.

CHAPTER EIGHT

area and continuing services in music

If educational institutions exist in order to help create values and behaviors needed by citizens in society, then the school doors must be kept open so that profitable interchange will occur between school and community. In providing useful services to its graduates and to its broader constituency, an educational institution not only seizes the opportunity to do a better job in meeting its students' needs, but also fulfills its proper role as an agent for the improvement of society.

The music program is a strong factor in school-community relationships and is especially sensitive to public expectations. This is because music is a live art and an aspect of human culture which transcends most barriers between age groups, sexes, races, and economic and social groups. Indeed, many school and college music programs are frankly conceived as vehicles for public relations, much to their detriment. The question becomes, how to use the music program to raise the public's level of musical taste and extend the benefits of musical participation, without exploiting and degrading music as sheer spectacle and casual entertainment.

The administrator needs to realize that, actually, programs of music education can scarcely be confined within the walls of an educational institution. The students will bring their music home and will practice and study it there, and their parents and friends will come to the school to hear them perform; the students will also form independent amateur groups and arrange their own performances. All of these activities will ultimately tell the tale of the school music program. That being the case, it is necessary to recognize the commitment of the music program as a force for music education within the community and surrounding area, and to aim for the most beneficial impact.

The program of area services has two sides—altruistic and selfish. While the school is seeking to enrich community life, it is at the same time required to explain and justify its program. It needs public opinion on its side, which means a continuing campaign to open up communications, to combat inertia, and to mold more positive attitudes. The music program holds a vital sector in this battle and the administrator must wisely guide the effort. This chapter thus deals with the music program as an agent in community services and with the employment of the media to this end. It will also deal with the music program's continuing responsibilities to its graduates in terms of job placement and continued contact through alumni services.

COMMUNITY SERVICES

The first and most obvious form of community service for any music program lies in bringing people to the school for musical activities. This means, first, sponsoring a strong series of concerts, clinics, conferences, and other appearances of interest to the public. Certain events may be directed at particular groups of people. For example, college and university music departments naturally wish to extend their message over a wide geographical area, and their primary audience includes the high school music teachers and their pupils; the university is especially concerned to provide help and example to these people, and at the same time, hopes to draw them within its orbit as a source of future students.

In setting up events that will be open to the public, therefore, it is highly important that their content is educationally and musically sound; the primary idea is never to entertain—although any good musical event may be enjoyable and entertaining—but to educate and inspire. This principle should apply to the audience as well as to any students who may be performing. The idea always is to focus upon the expressive nature of music in the attempt to extend musical understanding and to elevate musical tastes.

But it is fruitless to "go over the heads" of the audience; the level of the performers and of the audience must always be kept in mind. Not only must the performers be equal to the job, but the listeners also must sometimes be led step by step, over several seasons, to the acceptance of esoteric, *avant-garde* styles. Likewise, special events for special audiences—such as clinics for the various instruments, or lectures upon certain academic phases of music—need to be advertised as such and aimed directly at that particular clientele.

Besides musical events, a number of other occasions arise in which the public will visit school facilities. These include open house, parents' day, homecoming, workshops, recreational and athletic events, visits to museums, art exhibits, library, etc. Displays and live music are often appropriate at these functions and may be employed to inform and acquaint the visitors with the institution's music program.

In servicing those who contact and visit the institution, every effort must be made to handle them graciously and expeditiously. Guests, friends, and patrons of the institution deserve good telephone manners, a courteous reception, and prompt attention to their inquiries and complaints.

Many people, of course, do not choose to attend school events; if they are to be influenced at all, the music program must be brought to them. The primary means to such contact lies in appearances of the music students and faculty before local groups. The number of these groups is amazing, even in quite small communities. Below are just a few examples:

Types of Groups	*Examples*
educational	Parent-Teachers Association, Band Parents
civic	Rotary, Lions, Kiwanis
cultural	music clubs, literary societies
economic	chambers of commerce, labor unions
fraternal	Eagles, Elks, Masonic Lodge
political	League of Women Voters
patriotic	American Legion, DAR
professional	educational assn., medical assn.
religious	churches and related societies
welfare	Community Chest, United Fund
youth	YMCA, 4-H Club, Boy and Girl Scouts

Many of these groups like to have a good deal to say about how the local schools are run, and they may well include members of the school faculty among their membership. They also like to have music at their meetings and frequently call upon the schools to supply it. For such calls, the administrator needs to set policy to avoid overuse and exploitation of the students. At the same time, he is naturally anxious to respond constructively, using the occasion to give the students useful experience, while providing the host organization with the kind of music that will have a useful aesthetic impact and that will display the educational program to good advantage.

Of course, the individuals within these community groups are not all predisposed in favor of the schools or of the particular educational institution. They may not be especially fond of music. And, over the long-run, public opinion will prevail. So it is part of the job to bring public opinion to the side of education and music education, quietly and persistently, by all means available.

A more direct, hard-sell approach is often called for, especially by institutions of higher learning which have such a large and dispersed constituency. One factor in this effort is active participation of the music faculty in professional organizations. Activity of music student fraternities and pre-professional organizations can also be useful in this regard. Other important means of extending the service and influence of the institution are sending forth the performing groups on tour, and offering the services of faculty members as guest soloists, conductors, clinicians, and judges. Besides furnishing student teachers and consultant service to area schools, university music departments often set up research projects and pilot projects in promising locations. All this work is usually sparked by a regular program of school visitations by university music personnel, aimed at acquainting the area music students and their teachers with the musical activities and opportunities available through the university. Much of this activity relates to the recruitment of promising students, and serves to furnish them with information on career possibilities and financial assistance.

In addition to the more informal, sporadic activities which we have just discussed, schools and colleges often sponsor more sustained activities for teachers-in-service and other adults. These take the form of community orchestras, choruses, bands, and chamber groups, as well as Saturday and evening classes and summer workshops for credit. It is sometimes more convenient for interested clientele when these offerings are taken off campus and held in nearby locations. Administrative coordination is often provided by the institution's office of Extension or Adult Education, working in cooperation with the music unit.

COMMUNICATIONS

The various services performed by educational institutions presuppose a vast amount of person-to-person communication as the faculty work in and through local organizations and as they and their students appear before the public. But a special effort at communication is required. Public opinion is a product of custom and tradition, beliefs and values, the impact of real events, face to face discussions, opinions expressed by leaders or spokesmen, and the efforts of special interest groups. The mass media play a crucial role in disseminating these ideas and points of view. Any worthwhile program of area services, therefore, pays especial attention to communications and the dissemination of information within and from the institution.

Since all school personnel are spokesmen for the institution, good communication begins with adequate flow of information among students, teachers, and administrators. This may be accomplished via announcements to classes and student assemblies, faculty and student handbooks, faculty meetings, exchange of ideas within and among the various committees and councils, and regular bulletins, memos, and newsletters for students and faculty. Institutional catalogs are also a primary and authoritative source of information, useful both within the institution and to prospective students and other personnel needing detailed descriptive material.

Home contact materials are quite important to adequate communication. These include handbooks for parents, special publications, report cards and other information about the students' progress. These reports are designed to inform the parents directly of musical activities in which their children are participating, to outline objectives and opportunities, and to furnish advance notice of procedural detail required of the participating students. Without efforts in this direction, much may be lost "in translation," between the school, the students, and their parents.

Newspapers serve as the principal means of regular communication with the general public. This being the case, educational institutions usually designate an information officer to receive and prepare copy for the newspapers. This procedure tends toward more expertly prepared copy and better liaison with the newspapers; it also helps to ensure more equitable coverage of all phases of the school's music program and the various events sponsored by them.

The individual music teacher is not usually much concerned about news copy until an event approaches in which he is personally involved. Then he wants splashy headlines. He is usually disappointed because the announcement of standard music events is not ordinarily big news, and the newspapers so often bury these stories in the back pages. Sometimes they are overlooked entirely.

For routine announcement of musical events it is safer to rely upon bulletin boards, brochures and mailed announcements, and a listing of coming events on each concert program. One may also employ the newspapers' daily and weekly calendar of events, and regular paid advertisements. What will secure good coverage and reader interest are news stories and occasional feature stories with pictures, which relate notable happenings in the music program, such as contest results, gala events, the arrival of new equipment, honors and awards presented to students and teachers, and the like. Included within such stories may be announcements of forthcoming events.

News copy should be written in "reverse pyramid style"; all the important elements of the story are placed in the first paragraph, and each succeeding paragraph includes subsidiary detail of lesser importance. This allows the reader to grasp the main points and to decide whether to read further; it also enables the editor to trim the story from the bottom if he lacks space.

In news stories, quotations are good and the report's opinion is not good. Names of local participants are always important. It is wise to avoid technical terms and long sentences. The copy should be triple spaced, and the first page should begin about three inches from the top to allow room for adding the headline. The release date should be at top right and the writer's name and phone number at top left.

Those who are not experienced in journalistic writing usually find it best to release a precise summary of facts which the newspaper can employ in preparing their copy. Such information simply includes who, what, why, when, where, and how, along with the name and phone number of the one to contact for more information.

Newspaper reviews following major events are important in building interest toward ensuing appearances. If local newspapers do not send regular reviewers, reviews may be arranged with other qualified individuals and released to the news media.

Television appearances by large and small musical groups and by soloists, lecture and discussion programs, and music classes designed for television are excellent vehicles by which to carry the music program beyond institutional walls. Such presentations are especially suited to network stations of the public broadcasting system, and can sometimes be arranged on commercial channels as part of their public service time.

The difficulty with television lies in its merciless exposure of the performers, coupled with high production costs, which means extreme care and effort in setting up the programs. Participants must be ready for a long and exhausting session for technical purposes before the show finally goes on the air or is taped for later showing. But the impact and coverage of a good television production are usually great enough to warrant the effort.

Motion pictures and fine sound recordings are likewise demanding in terms of preparation and technical effort, but can be of tremendous value as educational and promotional devices. Radio programs and announcements also reach a large audience and are somewhat less complicated to produce. Various other types of material are suited to communication through posters, exhibits, brochures, slides, and film strips.

A complete and up to date mailing list is an important aid to good communications. This is used to mail regular calendars of musical events and alumni bulletins, and for special announcements of concerts, clinics and workshops, and the like. It is convenient if the general list can be subdivided into appropriate categories covering particular interests, so that only part of the list need be employed for events of a specialized character.

Needless to say, the image of an institution greatly depends upon the content and tone of the publications and information released by it. The Code of Ethics of the National Association of Schools of Music makes a point of this:

> *Article VII.* Institutional members shall not make exaggerated or misleading statements during interviews, auditions, nor in printed matter. All brochures, catalogs, and yearbooks shall be an accurate statement of the curriculum, objectives, equipment, and accommodations of the institution.
>
> *Article VIII.* Advertising shall be dignified and truthful.[1]

Of course, this same standard should be applied to all kinds and levels of schools. In the effort to whip up morale, to attract students and faculty, and to increase audiences, it is easy to exaggerate the accomplishments of the music program. Immediate results may seem rewarding, but will eventually result in a breakdown in public confidence. Administrators must not allow themselves or their coworkers to fall into this trap.

ALUMNI SERVICES

One of the most important services that any educational institution can render to its constituency is continued assistance to its graduates. In brief, it must offer its good offices toward the graduates' further educational activity, their placement in adequate jobs, and their continued participation in the affairs and concerns of the institution. Effective measures in these respects enlarge and strengthen the role of the institution.

---

[1] *Handbook, 1972,* National Association of Schools of Music, Washington, D.C., p. 19.

CONTINUATION OF SCHOOLING AND PARTICIPATION IN MUSIC

One of the primary responsibilities of any music program is to see that those students who are continuing in school are shepherded into the music program at the next level of schooling. Steps must be taken to ensure that members of the elementary school performing groups are acquainted with the junior high school music groups and their directors, and that these students are invited and urged to enroll in those groups at the proper time. This same process must occur when the students transfer to the high school. But a much greater effort is required at the point where students graduate from high school and seek entrance into college. To do the job properly here requires joint efforts from the high school and collegiate music faculties, under the direct encouragement of their respective administrators. The high school music faculty need to discuss the matter informally with their individual students, seeking to discover whether the student is bound for college, where he is likely to attend, and whether he expects to major in music. For their part, college music departments seek to bring high school music students to their campuses for musical events, and must assist and cultivate the area school music programs. Proper use of advertising and promotional mailings may extend this effort beyond the college's immediate area.

This process encourages the individual student to approach faculty members from the institution of his choice with questions about admission, music opportunities and requirements, and financial assistance where necessary. Where this sort of thing does not develop spontaneously, it may be stimulated by arranging career days and letters of referral by the high school music teachers.

A similar situation arises when college music students are completing their undergraduate programs and express an interest in graduate study. They deserve counseling on their qualifications, the kinds of graduate programs available, and where these are located. Assistance should be offered in terms of recommendations and help in completing procedures to secure admission.

JOB PLACEMENT

A strong placement service is a necessity for those who complete the music program and are seeking employment in a musical vocation. This is particularly true of collegiate institutions, since the high school diploma is not sufficient preparation for most musical vocations. Exceptions to this rule occur where native ability and circumstance may lead an individual to find employment as a singer or player in popular groups or some other aspect of show business; in the schools, also, an individual may secure enough preparation to launch a career in music within the armed services or in some phase of the music industry. But the vast majority of students who will be seeking musical employment are those who are approaching completion of their undergraduate or graduate music degrees and planning to work as music teachers, performers, conductors, or composers. The major responsibility for helping them find suitable work falls upon the college and university placement bureaus and music departments.

The demand for trained musicians changed drastically during the thirties and forties with the increasing use of radio and sound recordings. The consumption of live music for entertainment plummeted, and only a fraction of the former number of singers, players, and conductors could be employed. These jobs have since fallen to the few who performed for radio and who cut the recordings. The advent of television has done little to change that picture.

Simultaneously, music programs in schools and colleges developed at a rapid rate, requiring more music teachers and thus absorbing the vast majority of those who wished to follow a musical vocation. True, many of these individuals were also able to function as professional performers, conductors, and composers, but this has been generally possible only as supplementary work or moonlighting. In short, many teachers have filled part-time posts with community symphonies and church choirs, or have done their composing, research, and recitals as members of university faculties. One could always count on finding a position somewhere teaching music.

This situation is now being threatened by a flattening out of school enrollments, inadequate financing of schools, and an increase in "the number of graduates prepared to teach . . . from 26.7% (in 1950) to 36.2% (in 1971) of all graduates receiving the bachelor's and first professional degree."[2] This has finally resulted in an actual surplus of qualified applicants for open positions as teachers in the schools. Figure 1 illustrates how the problem is likely to grow.[3] It shows that the long period of teacher shortage was passed in 1969 when 111 qualified graduates competed for each 100 open teaching positions, and by 1979 it is expected that nearly 274 graduates will be available for each 100 open positions. Obviously, a teaching certificate can no longer be considered a cheap form of unemployment insurance.

---

[2] William S. Graybeal, "Teacher Surplus and Teacher Shortage," *Phi Delta Kappan,* 53, no. 2 (Oct. 1971), 84.

[3] *Ibid.,* p. 83.

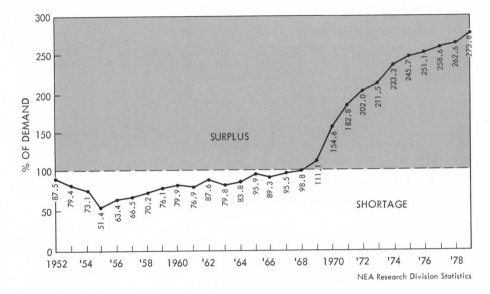

Figure 1. Supply of Beginning Teachers as Percent of Normal Demand, 1952 to 1979, According to Present Trends. From NEA Research Division Statistics. Used by permission.

However, this situation can be viewed in another way. During the long period of teacher shortage, the schools were forced to overload instructors. Maximum elementary class sizes have been figured at 34 pupils per elementary classroom and 199 pupils per day in the secondary schools. More defensible maximums of 24 pupils per elementary classroom and 124 pupils per day in secondary schools would roughly absorb the projected teacher production. If the extra teaching positions can be funded, the situation can result in reduced teacher-pupil ratios and improved education; this would require that a major share of any increased school revenues must be reserved for this purpose.

It is already apparent that most school music programs are understaffed. Without figures to prove it, it is clear that most school music teachers, working to capacity, are unable to fill the demand for more instruction. The number of special music teachers for the elementary schools is so grossly inadequate that classroom teachers are being forced to teach a subject for which they are not prepared, and in many instances daily music instruction has simply been abandoned. Similarly, many instrumental instructors are forced to test the volunteers as a means of selecting the number of students they will have time to instruct. Most schools, indeed, are not able to start or to continue instruction in the stringed instruments because enough qualified string teachers cannot be found. Many university music faculties, too, still possess only a fraction of the number of people with doctorates that are required in order to staff their programs of advanced study.

On the basis of information compiled in the Directory of Music Faculties in Colleges and Universities of the United States and Canada, published each biennium by the College Music Society, it is possible to pinpoint precise ratios in regard to the latest trends in staffing patterns for music in higher education. Over 13,000 faculty positions are listed in the 1970–72 Directory. Less than 3,000 of these (2,832 in the United States) are filled by persons who have earned the doctorate. The following chart illustrates the general distribution:

	Staff holding doctorates	*Master's*	*Other*
No. of positions	2,832	7,382	3,552
%'s	20.5%	53.6%	25.9%

Total number of positions listed: 13,766

The upshot of the situation is that music education is faced with a period during which teaching qualifications will be gradually raised and faculties will be slowly enlarged, and the more qualified graduates will have a greater competitive edge. University music administrators will need to take steps toward greater selectivity of entering music majors, enriched curricula, and more vigorous efforts in placing their graduates.

The value of effective placement service is threefold. First, it fulfills one of the primary objectives of the music students and of the institution, in that their study will result in a marketable skill. Secondly, well-placed graduates will have a powerful impact upon the music programs and cultural life of the area, where most of them will tend to remain at least for a time—and upon the musical profession and musical life of the nation generally. Finally, well-placed graduates enhance the reputation and drawing power of the institution. Some music schools are in an enviable situation simply because so many of their graduates have gone to positions where they are able to send back their top students to their alma mater for advanced training.

The placement bureau which exists in most universities will ordinarily contact those students who are in their final year, to secure their registration. Forms are supplied on which the students outline their personal and professional data, and other forms are distributed to secure recommendations from their major professors. These materials are filed for referral to interested employers. Job notices are received by this agency and posted or directly referred to the individual. A similar procedure is followed by the commercial placement agencies who charge a commission of those whom they have assisted in securing positions. But this process is likely to be perfunctory, due to the lack of personal contact and attention. Special assistance from the music department is required.

In the first place, students do not always know how to present their qualifications in the strongest way. The forms are not sufficiently detailed nor flexible. Thus, the student requires guidance in preparing an adequate profile of his qualifications. Secondly, many employers bypass the large placement bureaus because these do not really know the candidates; they approach the music department, or an acquaintance within it, for more direct recommendations. These inquiries are, of course, relayed to the official placement bureau, but are also referred directly to the most qualified candidates. They may ask counsel regarding the pros and cons of the particular position, and, if they decide to pursue it, the weight of further recommendations by telephone or by letter may be added. In short, departmental effort naturally results in a better match between the available jobs and the candidates, increases the confidence of the employer in such candidates, and promotes a sense of joint responsibility and trust among employers, candidates, and the music department which acts as broker.

Placement service, of course, is not confined to the year of graduation; it should also be available for new referrals and recommendations during as many years as the individual maintains active contact. For their part, graduates should be encouraged to inform the department when they plan to move, so that new candidates may be referred to those jobs.

Administrative involvement in the placement effort is important. Several large universities and conservatories maintain full-fledged music placement offices. But smaller ones can rely upon some individual to serve as placement officer on a part-time basis, if he is provided the means to discharge this function. In many institutions it will be the music executive himself, who keeps an active file handy to his phone for immediate response to inquiries.

Adult Education and Musical Activity

A good many of the products of a secondary school or collegiate music program do not proceed directly with further schooling or require job placement in music. They may, however, remain interested in music as an avocation, and the music department must certainly help provide appropriate opportunities for those who remain within reaching distance.

This effort is typically informal, since the music staff will ordinarily be found conducting or participating in local community orchestras, bands, church choirs, dance bands, chamber ensembles, opera and concert associations, and music clubs. From this vantage point, they can make sure that an invitation is left open to the graduates, along with other musicians of the community, to participate in accordance with their interests and talents. In addition, these alumni must be kept informed of opportunities for additional music study without pursuing a degree, through the Saturday and evening classes and summer workshops which may be sponsored by the institution.

ALUMNI CONTACT

The final responsibility of an institution to its alumni lies in retaining active contact and exchange with them. Over a period of years, these individuals spread far and wide and many will attain positions of considerable effect and influence. The alumni, after all, are the chief exhibits of the quality of a music program and can provide a useful example and encouragement to the current students. If properly cultivated, they will retain an interest in their alma mater and can be counted upon to support and defend its program.

Much of the total effort in area service will naturally relate to those alumni who remain in the area. They will attend musical events on campus. They may participate in local music groups and other activities being sponsored by the institution. They will certainly be found among the audience when music programs are presented before local groups and when representatives of the music program appear in other localities, on tour or in the capacity of clinicians, contest judges, consultants, and the like. They will follow the musical activities of the music department as these are presented on radio and television and reported in the newspapers and professional journals. Eventually, as parents of students who are perhaps enrolled in the 'same institution, they will again be specifically concerned with the quality and extent of music instruction as it affects their own children, and will thus take a direct part in evaluating and supporting that program. In one sense, therefore, the alumni simply become an integral part of the larger community which any educational system serves.

But the alumni are also a special group, who want their institution and its music program to succeed since they are creatures of it and because they are proud to be identified with a thriving institution. Some are more concerned and demonstrative than others, but all are at least curious.

All educational institutions thus maintain some form of alumni contact. There will be annual homecoming events, often an alumni bulletin, and perhaps an organized alumni association. Contributions will often be solicited from the alumni for special causes or continuing needs.

The music alumni are a special group within a group, because they were a somewhat unique group of students. Like athletics, music is a team undertaking. Members of school performing organizations learned to devote themselves to the group. They also got to know one another very well. And those who majored in music had to put most of their energies into that program—more so than students in most of the other disciplines. Consequently, a community feeling usually arises among serious music students which transcends the walls of the institution. After graduation they retain an interest in the activities of their former classmates, their former teachers, and the development of the music program.

To satisfy this natural interest and loyalty, and to turn it to the benefit of the current music program, it is useful to make a special effort to maintain relations with the music alumni of an institution. Although a lot of interchange will occur anyway, on an informal basis, the music executive needs to provide for a deliberate program of alumni relations. Either he or an appointed officer should build a file of all music alumni for whom records can be found; this should include surname and married name, major field of music and degree, year of graduation, positions held, and current address. Special newsletters or bulletins should be occasionally addressed to these people, with return cards to procure news and changes of address. Special invitations should be issued for particular concerts or events where the alumni may gather together; these may include the regular school homecoming, a large music educators convention, or the year's largest musical event.

The effort to engage the interest of music alumni can be productive. It can result in contributions to a music scholarship fund or to the purchase of buildings and equipment. It can help bring more students into the music program. Through questionnaires and discussion it can help to clarify the problems of the music program and to suggest curricular revisions. But such concrete results are often not forthcoming. What good alumni relations always does is to improve the perspective of the current faculty and students and to serve as a bulwark of the public's attitude. The attitude of the general public toward a music program is largely conditioned by the attitudes and activities of those who underwent it; they will certainly not respect any educational institution which has no concern with its products, who, in their turn, do not care to be identified with it.

Indeed, it is especially fitting to close a book, which is addressed to the matter of administration in music education, with the topic of music alumni. After all, the function of administration was to provide the means to the instruction of those students. The administrator's work in building a curriculum, developing and working with the faculty and student body, securing space and equipment, and handling the financial and organizational details of the operation is all directed at producing the best possible graduates who will help to increase the musical stature of the nation. Regardless of his final reputation, its actual measure must rest primarily upon the accomplishments of those students who were once in his charge.

QUESTIONS FOR DISCUSSION

1. Why is interchange between school and community important? What outcomes should be sought?

2. What benefits should accrue from a vigorous effort to bring the public to school musical events? May the public be entertained and educated at the same time?

3. What avenues are appropriate for bringing the school's music program to those who do not attend events at the school?

4. How is good communication promoted among school personnel? How may newspapers and the other media be effectively employed to extend the interchange among school and community?

5. What opportunities and forms of encouragement may be offered to musical adults to continue their musical and educational activity?

6. Does the music unit have a legitimate role to play in assisting its graduates to find employment? What seem to be the current and future trends in the employment of musicians?

7. What are the ordinary avenues for retaining significant contact with a school's music alumni? What values may obtain?

SUGGESTED READINGS

Fine, Benjamin, and Vivienne Anderson, *The School Administrator and the Press.* New London, Conn.: Arthur C. Croft Publications, 1956.

Grinnell, J. W., and Raymond J. Young, *The School and the Community.* New York: The Ronald Press, 1955.

Jones, James J., *School Public Relations.* New York: The Center for Applied Research in Education, Inc., 1966.

Kindred, Leslie W., *School Public Relations.* Englewood Cliffs, N.J.: Prentice-Hall, Inc., 1957.

Macomber, F. Glenn, and Albert L. Ayars, "Home Town Becomes a Classroom," *School Executive,* 74:41–44 (August, 1955).

Yeager, William A., *School-Community Relations.* New York: The Dryden Press, 1951.

index

Academic tenure, 89–90
Accountability of administrator, 29
Accounting, financial, 127–29
Acoustics, 134–38
Admissions, criteria for, 99
Adult education, 161–62
Advertising for faculty, 78–79
Advisement of students, 68–69, 98–102
Alumni services, 156–64
  adult education and activity, 161–62
  contact, 163–64
  continuation of schooling and partici-
    pation, 157
  job placement, 157–61
Applicants, faculty, screening of, 79–80
Applied music, 61–63
Assignment, faculty, 81–82
Assistant instructors, 88
Assistant professors, 88–89
Associate professors, 88–89
Attendance laws, 93
Audio/visual services, 66
Auditoriums, 138

Authority of administrator, 29–30
Awards, 106

Bachelor of Arts degree, 60
Bachelor of Music Education (degree pro-
    gram), 59
Band directors, administrative role of, 41
Band Parents' Club, 18
Band uniforms, 145
Barnard, Chester, 15
Basic Music (degree program), 60
Behavior, student, 93–94, 104–106
Board of Regents, administrative role of,
    35
Board of Trustees, administrative role of,
    2, 35
Budgets, 117–25
  administration, 124–25
  form of, 117–22
  preparation, 122–24
Building principals, administrative role
    of, 1, 38
Busing, 10–11

California Supreme Court, 114
Carnegie Corporation, 6
Chairman, 39–40
Chancellor, administrative role of, 1, 35–36
Child labor laws, 93
Choir robes, 145
Civilian Conservation Corps, 113
Classes:
  scheduling, 66–68
  size, 159
Classrooms, 140
College Music Society, 13, 79, 160
Colleges, 13–14
  advisement and counseling, 101, 102
  curriculums, 13, 58–65, 93
  enrollment, 93, 97–98
  faculty assignment, 82
  financing, 112–13, 115
  music programs, 3
  placement bureaus, 158–60
  recruiting ethics, 97–98
  See also Universities
Committee of Ten, The, 5
Committee on the Reorganization of Secondary Education, 5–6
Communication:
  faculty, 83–85
  services and, 153–56
  student, 94, 104–106
Community colleges, 13, 59
Community services, 151–53
Comprehensive Musicianship (course), 61
Compulsory school attendance laws, 93
Contemporary Music Project, 61
Control, administrative, 31–33
Cooperative Research Program (1954), 114
Coordinator of Curriculum Services, 21, 39–40
Copying service, 104
Counseling of students, 68–69, 98–102
Curriculums, 47–75
  defined, 47–48
  evaluation of, 71–73
  expediting instruction, 65–71
    arranging public events, 69–70
    class scheduling, 66–68
    equipment, 65–66, 144–47
    office aids, 70
    student advisement and counseling, 68–69, 98–102

Curriculums (*cont.*)
    supervisory services, 71
    teaching space, 65–66, 141–43
  objectives, 48–53
    formulating, 51–53
    levels of, 49–50
  offerings and requirements, 53–65
    colleges, 13, 58–65, 93
    elementary schools, 53–55
    public schools, 93
    secondary schools, 55–58

Davis, Ralph Currier, 31–32
Dean, 1
Dean of Fine Arts, administrative role of, 36–38
Decentralization, 30–31
Degree programs, 59–60, 64
Department chairmen, 2
Director, 39–40
Directors of Music, administrative role of, 21, 40–41, 63
Directory of Music Faculties in Colleges and Universities of the United States and Canada (College Music Society), 13, 79, 160
Districting, school, 11–12
Doctoral degrees, 13, 64
Doctor of Arts, 64

Economic Opportunity Act (1964), 114
Educational Policies Committee, 6
Education and Professional Development Act (1965), 114
Elementary and Secondary Education Act (1965), 114
Elementary schools, 9
  class sizes, 159
  curriculums, 53–55
  districting, 11–12
  faculty assignment, 82
  faculty recruitment, 78–79
  non-public, 12–13
  student promotion policy, 100
Eliot, Charles W., 5
Employee protection, 129–31
Enrollment, 93, 97–98
Equipment, 65–66, 144–47
European schools, 57
Evaluation:
  curriculum, 71–73

Evaluation (*cont.*)
faculty, 85–90
fellow faculty reports, 86
merit raises, 87–88
observation of instruction, 86
polls of students, 86
promotion in rank, 88–89
public performance, 86
single salary schedule and, 80–81, 87
tenure, 89–90
tests, 86
student, 107–109
Executives, administrative role of:
institutional, 35–36
music, 38–40

Facilities, 133–49
equipment, 65–66, 144–47
maintenance, 146–48
music rooms, 134–41
acoustics, 134–38
auditoriums, 138
classrooms, 140
laboratories, 140
location, 134–38
offices, 140
practice rooms, 103, 139–40, 144–45
rehearsal rooms, 138–39, 145
special facilities, 141
studios, 140
planning new, 143–44
space, utilizing and securing, 65–66, 141–43
use of, 146–48
Faculty, 76–91
administration, relations with, 16–17
administrative role of, 24–25, 40–41
assignment, 81–82
communication, 83–85
evaluation, 85–90
fellow faculty reports, 86
merit raises, 87–88
observation of instruction, 86
polls of students, 86
promotion in rank, 88–89
public performance, 86
single salary schedule and, 87
tenure, 89–90
tests, 86
maintenance of facilities and, 147
marks and, 107–109
morale, 83–85

Faculty (*cont.*)
orientation, 82–83
recruitment and selection, 77–81
advertising the opening, 78–79
interviews, 80
job description, 77–78
the offer, 80–81
screening applicants, 79–80
shortage of, 158–60
supervisory service, 71
Faculty Handbook Index, 84
Fayol, Henri, 14
Federal agencies:
administrative role of, 33–34
financing and, 113–15
Federal Surplus Commodities Corporation, 113
Financing, 112–17
students and, 96–98
Fiscal management, 111–32
accounting, 127–29
budgets, 117–25
administration, 124–25
form of, 117–22
preparation, 122–24
employee protection, 129–31
financing, 112–17
funds, protection of, 129–31
goods and services, procuring of, 125–27
property protection, 129–31
Floating periods, 68
Follett, Mary Parker, 14
Foundation Program, 113
Foundations and Principles of Music Education (Leonhard and House), 52
Fraternal organizations, 105
Funds, protection of, 129–31
Furnishings, 144

G. I. Bill (1944), 113
General music (course), 55
Goods, procuring of, 125–27
Governing boards, administrative role of, 2, 10, 34–35
Graduate programs, 64–65, 108
Griffiths, Daniel E., 15
Group life insurance, 130
Gulick, Luther, 14

Head (title), 39–40

Higher Education Act (1965), 114
Higher Education Facilities Act (1963), 114
High schools, 9
  advisement and counseling, 69, 101
  continuation of schooling and, 157
  districting, 11–12

Institutional executives, administrative role of, 35–36
Instruction, 20–21
  expedition of, 65–71
    advisement and counseling, 68–69, 98–102
    arranging public events, 69–70
    class scheduling, 66–68
    equipment, 65–66, 144–47
    office aids, 70
    supervisory service, 71
    teaching space, 65–66
  observation of, 86
Instructors, 88–89
Instruments:
  providing of, 102–103
  selection of, 145
Insulation, of music rooms, 135
Insurance, 130
Interviews, faculty, 80
Introduction to Music (course), 58

Job description, 77–78
Job placement, 157–61
Johns, Roe L., 15–16, 112–13
Junior colleges, 13, 59, 99

Laboratories, 140
Leadership:
  administrative, 41–45
  natural selection, 42
  traits, listing of, 42–43
Lecturers, 88
Liability insurance, 130
Libraries, 66, 103–104
Line and staff concept, 24–28
Local governing boards, administrative role of, 2, 10, 34–35

Mailing lists, 156
Maintenance of facilities, 146–48
Management process, 21–33
  control, 31–33

Management process (*cont.*)
  organizing, 24–30
  planning, 22–24, 143–44
Manpower Development and Training Act (1962), 114
Marks, 107–109
Morale, faculty, 83–85
Morphet, Edgar L., 15–16, 112–13
Morrill Act (1862), 113
Mort, Paul, 15
Motion pictures, 155
Music, applied, 61–63
Musical Performance (degree program), 60
Music appreciation (course), 55
Music Consultant, 21
Music executives, administrative role of, 38–40
Musicianship, promoting of, 106–107
Music literature (course), 61
Music programs, 3–4, 20–46
  administrative roles, 33–45
    building principals, 1, 38
    Dean of Fine Arts, 36–38
    federal and state agencies, 33–34
    institutional executives, 35–36
    leadership and, 41–45
    local governing boards, 2, 10, 34–35
    music executives, 38–40
    music teachers, 24–25, 40–41
  instruction, 20–21
  management process, 21–33
    control, 31–33
    organizing, 24–30
    planning, 22–24, 143–44
  supervision, 21, 31–33
Music rooms, 134–41
  acoustics, 134–38
  auditoriums, 138
  classrooms, 140
  laboratories, 140
  location, 134–38
  offices, 140
  practice rooms, 103, 139–40, 144–45
  rehearsal rooms, 138–39, 145
  special facilities, 141
  studios, 140
Music Supervisor, 21
Music teachers. *See* Faculty
Music theory (course), 61
Music understanding (course), 58

National Assessment of Educational Progress, 6–8, 50
National Association of Schools of Music, 13–14, 60, 79
By-Laws and Regulations, 59
Code of Ethics, 98, 156
National Defense Education Act (1958), 114
National Education Association (NEA), 5–6, 11
National Science Foundation (1950), 114
National Youth Administration, 113
Newspapers, 154–55
Norton, John K., 15

Objectives of curriculums, 48–53
formulating, 51–53
levels, 49–50
Offerings, curriculum, 53–65
colleges, 13, 58–65, 93
elementary schools, 53–55
secondary schools, 55–58
Office aids, 70
Offices, 140
Operational control, 32
Organization, structural, 24–30
Orientation, faculty, 82–83

Parent-Teacher Association, 18
Performing groups, 56–58
Personal objectives, 50
Placement services, 78–79, 157–61
Planning, 22–24, 143–44
Planning-Programming-Budgeting Systems (P.P.B.S.), 120, 122
Policy-making, 23–24
Polls, student, 86
Population, student, 92–95
Practice rooms, 103, 139–40, 144–45
Pre-school education, 13
Presidents, university, 1, 3
administrative role of, 23, 35–36
Principals, building, administrative role of, 1, 38
Professional programs, 60
Professors, 88–89
Program objectives, 50
Promotion:
faculty, 88–89
student, 100

Property protection, 129–31
Public events, arranging, 69–70
Public schools, 10–12
curriculums, 93
districting, 11–12
enrollment, 93
financing, 112–15
public event sponsoring, 69–70
Purchasing agents, 125–26
Purposes of Education in American Democracy (Educational Policies Committee), 6, 49

Radio programs, 155–56
Raises, merit, 87–88
Rank, promotion in, 88–89
Records, student, 109
Recruitment:
ethics, 97–98
faculty, 77–81
advertising the opening, 78–79
interviews, 80
job description, 77–78
the offer, 80–81
screening applicants, 79–80
student, 95–98
Rehearsal rooms, 138–39, 145
Requirements, curriculum, 53–65
colleges, 58–65
elementary schools, 53–55
secondary schools, 55–58
Resource services, 102–104
Responsibility of administration, 28–29
Roller, Theodore L., 15–16
Rotating periods, 68

Scheduling of classes, 66–68
Scholarship, promoting of, 106–107
Scholarships, 24, 97, 99
School boards:
administrative role of, 2, 10, 34–35
financing and, 113
School Building Authority, 116
School codes, 34–35
School executive officer, administrative role of, 35
Schooling:
college, 13–14
continuation of, 157
function of, 4–10

Schooling (*cont.*)
  pre-school education, 13
  types and levels, 10–14
  university, 13–14
Schools. *See* Elementary schools; High
  schools; Secondary schools; Public
  schools
School superintendent, administrative
  role of, 1, 23, 35–36
Screening of applicants, 79–80
Secondary schools:
  advisement and counseling, 101
  class scheduling, 67
  class size, 159
  curriculums, 55–58
  districting, 11–12
  faculty assignment, 82
  faculty recruitment, 78–79
  non-public, 12–13
Security of facilities, 146
Services, 150–65
  alumni, 156–64
    adult education and activity, 161–62
    contact, 163–64
    continuation of schooling, 157
    job placement, 157–61
  audio/visual, 66
  communications and, 153–56
  community, 151–53
  copying, 104
  placement, 78–79, 157–61
  procuring of, 125–27
  resource, 102–104
  supervisory, 71
Seven Cardinal Principles of Education,
  6, 49
Simon, Herbert, 15
Single salary schedule, 80–81, 87
Smith-Hughes Act (1917), 113
Smith-Lever Act (1914), 113
Solo preparation, 57
Sound recordings, 155
Space, utilizing and securing, 65–66, 141–43
Special education, 100
Stanford University, 67
State agencies:
  administrative role of, 33–34
  financing and, 113–15
State Offices of Education, 33
State Superintendents of Public Instruc-
  tion, 33

Students, 92–110
  administration, relations with, 17
  advisement and counseling, 68–69, 98–102
  beginning instruction opportunities,
    95–96
  behavior, 93–94, 104–106
    official code for, 105–106
  communication, 94, 104–106
  enrollment trends, 93
  evaluation of, 107–109
  financing, 96–98
  polls, 86
  population, 92–95
  promotion policy and, 100
  psychological needs, 94–95
  records, 109
  recruitment for music, 95–98
  resource services, 102–104
  scholarship and musicianship,
    promoting of, 106–107
  scholarships, 24, 97, 99
Studios, 140
Supervision, 21, 31–33
Supervisors, music, 1, 21
Supervisory service, 71

Taylor, Frederic, 14
Teachers. *See* Faculty
Television, 155
Tenure, academic, 89–90
Tests, faculty, 86
Texas public schools, financing systems
  of, 114–15
Textbooks, 66
Tracking, 100

Undergraduate programs, 58–64
United States Department of Defense,
  118, 120
United States Department of Health,
  Education, and Welfare, 33
United States Office of Education, 3, 6,
  33, 118
Universities, 13–14
  admissions, 99
  advisement and counseling, 69, 102
  degree programs, 59–60, 64
  departmental organization, 27
  faculty assigment, 82
  financing, 115
  graduate programs, 64–65

Universities *(cont.)*
  insurance, 130
  marks, 108
  musicianship, promoting of, 107
  placement bureaus, 78–79, 158, 160–61
  promotion in rank, 88–89
  public event sponsoring, 69–70
  re-centralization of authority, 30
  recruiting ethics, 97–98
  undergraduate programs, 58–64
University chancellor, administrative role
  of, 35–36

University governing board, administrative role of, 35
University presidents, 1, 3
  administrative role of, 23, 35–36
University teachers, administrative role
  of, 41

Vocational Education Act (1963), 114

Works Progress Administration, 113
World Almanac (1970), 13